"Donne [was] one of [the] preme[nt intelligent] poets i[n the] English language, he was also the first Englishman to write verse in a way that reflected the whole complex activity of intelligence."

In all of Donne's poetry there is paradox, humor, emotion and analysis; his devices of irony and psychological probing combined with passion and sensibility produced a body of work that remains one of the richest and most original in the language.

A. Alvarez evaluates this body of work, along with the work of other metaphysical poets, as he discusses the poets in the context of their time, and their importance throughout the history of English poetry. The author tells how the metaphysical poets were dismissed by the Restoration writers and critically attacked by Dr. Ben Jonson and the Fellows of the Royal Society, who accused their work of "medievalism."

That the metaphysical poets were the most modern of English poets, the author proves in a thoroughly intriguing and persuasive study—a study that shows how the poetry of the school of Donne remains vital, urgent and meaningful for the 20th century.

THE
SCHOOL OF
DONNE

A. ALVAREZ

A MENTOR BOOK

Published by The New American Library,
New York and Toronto
The New English Library Limited, London

FIRST PRINTING, JANUARY, 1967

MENTOR BOOKS are published *in the United States* by
The New American Library, Inc.,
in Canada by The New American Library of Canada Limited,
295 King Street East, Toronto 2, Ontario,
in the United Kingdom by The New English Library Limited,
Barnard's Inn, Holborn, London, E.C. 1, England

PRINTED IN THE UNITED STATES OF AMERICA

To
Ursula

Language most shewes a man: speake that I may see thee. It springs out of the most retired, and inmost parts of us, and is the Image of the Parent of it, the mind. No glasse renders a mans forme, or likenesse, so true as his speech. Nay, it is likened to a man; and as we consider feature, and composition in a man; so words in Language: in the greatnesse, aptnesse, sound, structure, and harmony of it.

Ben Jonson, from Vives

The proprieties and delicacies of the English are known to few; 'tis impossible even for a good wit to understand and practise them, without the help of a liberal education, long reading, and digesting of those few good authors we have amongst us, the knowledge of men and manners, the freedom of habitudes and conversation with the best company of both sexes; and, in short, without wearing off the rust which he has contracted while he was laying in a stock of learning.

John Dryden

Thou hast . . . open'd Us a Mine
Of rich and pregnant phansie, drawne a line
Of masculine expression. . . .

Thomas Carew on Donne

CONTENTS

ACKNOWLEDGMENTS

THIS book is substantially the text of six lectures delivered to the Christian Gauss Seminars in Criticism at Princeton University in the spring of 1958. I would like to thank all the members of the seminar for their patience and criticism, but above all R. P. Blackmur and E. B. O. Borgerhoff, whose original invitation to give the lectures forced me to complete a book I had been postponing a long time. I am also immensely indebted to F. W. Bateson, who, without agreeing with a word of it, read the final manuscript and offered innumerable suggestions for its improvement. My thanks, too, to the Rockefeller Foundation, particularly to John Marshall and R. W. July of the Humanities Division, who gave me a generous grant which helped me prepare the book for publication.

The original work was begun under the supervision of Miss Helen Gardner. My debt to her in the first chapter will be obvious to anyone who knows her authoritative work on the subject. I acknowledge it gratefully. I would also like to thank the President and Fellows of Corpus Christi College, Oxford, the Goldsmiths' Company and the Jane Eliza Procter Foundation of Princeton University for the various grants and fellowships which made possible my initial research into the subject. I am also very grateful to Miss Rosellen Brown and Miss Sherna Steinberg of Brandeis University who devoted a great deal of time to typing and checking the anthology.

In order to keep the footnotes to a manageable size, I have given the references only of prose quotations and of such verse as has not been reprinted since the seventeenth century. The rest of the poetry is quoted, wherever possible, from the definitive texts, nearly all of which, except Cowley's, are published by the Oxford University Press.

Chapter V has appeared in *The Hudson Review* and some of the material in Chapter I was broadcast in the B.B.C. Third Programme and printed in *The Listener*.

INTRODUCTION

THE purpose of this book is, first and last, critical.
I say that straight away, since, obviously, a certain
amount of scholarship is involved in any study of this
kind, and this particular book began life in the early 'fifties
with the most honourable academic intentions. But the original research got put aside and finally abandoned. The bulk
of it survives as a silent background for the criticism, although I have added an appendix to back up some of the
assertions in the first chapter, and in the last have extended
my critical thesis into the history of ideas. For the rest, I
have tried to omit all detail that is not strictly to the critical
point and have kept the references to secondary works to a
minimum. As a result, I hope the book will be of as much
interest to the literary layman as to the specialist.

It may perhaps seem a little late in the day to be writing
about the Metaphysicals. The great vogue for Donne passed
with the passing of the Anglo-American experimental movement in modern poetry. But for that reason it is now easier
to see Donne's work as major poetry in its own right rather
than, as was once the fashion, as a first rough draft for the
poems of T. S. Eliot. For example, even a valuable, thorough study of the Metaphysicals' background like R. L.
Sharp's *From Donne to Dryden* talks about the poetry itself
in terms of a tortured groping more applicable to Hart
Crane than to John Donne. Neither this critical mannerism
nor the reaction against it—led by Miss Rosemond Tuve
and devoted to proving that Donne differed hardly at all
from any other Renaissance poet—does justice to his originality or influence.

Criticism is always partial, it always reflects the preoccupations of the time in which it was written. So I make no
claims at all to present a final image of Donne here. What
I am trying to do is to show how Donne affected the language and form of poetry in a way that is still peculiarly
meaningful for us, and is rapidly becoming yet more meaningful. There are, of course, few more melancholy sights
than that of the literary critic who leaves whatever he can

do to pronounce on the state of man. So I would like simply to invoke the witness of Miss Hannah Arendt's profound analysis of *The Human Condition* in which, with immense authority, she argues for the urgency of the intelligence as the only possible alternative to the anonymous labouring processes of mass society. This book is an attempt to define a kind of intelligence which, though it was first expressed at the end of the sixteenth century, is still vital and urgent.

For Donne was not only one of the most supremely intelligent poets in the language, he was also the first Englishman to write verse in a way that reflected the whole complex activity of intelligence. A number of Elizabethan poets embodied the philosophical truths of their period in verse of considerable elegance and power. But Donne created a poetic language of thought, a mode of expression which so took for granted the intellectual tone and preoccupations of his time that it made of them, as it were, the stage on which the intimate give-and-take of personal poetry was played. He was, in short, the first intellectual realist in poetry.

Eliot first made much the same point as early as 1923 in an article that has, to my knowledge, never been reprinted:

> One of the characteristics of Donne which wins him, I fancy, his interest for the present age, is his fidelity to emotion as he finds it; his recognition of the complexity of feeling and its rapid alterations and antitheses. A change of feeling, with Donne, is rather the regrouping of the same elements under a mood which was previously subordinate: it is not the substitution of one mood for a wholly different one. . . . There are two ways in which we may find a poet to be modern: he may have made a statement which is true everywhere and for all time . . ., or there may be an accidental relationship between his mind and our own. The latter is a fashion. . . . The age of Donne, and the age of Marvell, are sympathetic to us, and it demands a considerable effort of dissociation to decide to what degree we are deflected towards him by a local or temporary bias. . . . The age objects to the heroic and the sublime, and it objects to the simplification and separation of the mental faculties. The objections are largely well grounded, and react against the nineteenth century; they are partly—how far I do not inquire—the

product of the popularization of the study of mental phenomena. Ethics having been eclipsed by psychology, we accept the belief that any state of mind is extremely complex, and chiefly composed of odds and ends in constant flux manipulated by desire and fear. When, therefore, we find a poet who neither suppresses nor falsifies, and who expresses complicated states of mind, we give him welcome. And when we find his poetry containing everywhere potential or actual wit, our thirst has been relieved . . . Neither the fantastic (Clevelandism is becoming popular) nor the cynical nor the sensual occupies an excessive importance with Donne; the elements of his mind had an order and congruity. The range of his feelings was great, but no more remarkable than its unity. He was altogether present in every thought and in every feeling. . . . Our appreciation of Donne must be an appreciation of what we lack, as well as of what we have in common with him.[1]

The difference between the time at which Eliot wrote this and our own lies in the way in which psychology can now be taken more or less for granted. The complexity and contradictoriness of the emotions are no longer fighting subjects. Instead, the contemporary problem is to write with an intelligence that recognizes this complexity and controls it in all its baffling fragmentariness.

Eliot's insights into Donne's originality were largely sidetracked by later critics in their search for a technique to produce certain effects. Hence the inordinate concentration on the 'outlandish conceit', as though the whole of Metaphysical poetry were reducible to a single, rather ostentatious trick of style. I simply want to replace the stress on the element of realism in Donne, the skill by which he created a poetic language in which technique was at the service of a fullness of the intelligence.

Nowadays 'realism' usually means a certain wilful harping on the facts of life, an insistence on the short, frank word and the daringly, or drearily, sordid detail. There is, of course, an element of this kind of frankness in Donne's poetry, but, as often as not, it enters when he is most classical: in, say, "Elegie XIX. Going to Bed", where he is being a kind of new English Ovid. The realism I am referring to is, however, something more diffused and its effect is

[1] 'John Donne', *The Nation and Athenaeum*, xxxiii, 1923, pp. 331-2.

distinctly not of grinding the reader's nose into the dirt. On the contrary, the final impression is one of a peculiarly heightened dignity.

This sense of personal dignity is at the center of Donne's work. At the simplest level, it is his perennial theme:

> She'is all States, and all Princes, I,
> Nothing else is.

is an extreme but typical way of putting it. This dignity measures his distance from the more conventional Elizabethans, as I try to show in the first chapter, and, as I suggest in the sixth, it is at the root of his "masculine", "strong" style. More important, it makes for the cohesion of his work, that unity and strength which give his collected poems an importance difficult to pin down in any single one of them. He is, after all, one of the few major poets before this century whose achievement is not summed up in any one really extended work.

Yet despite this unity there is considerable variation in his style. The *Elegies*, for example, seem definably younger work than the best *Songs and Sonets*. This is due to something more than their occasional self-consciousness, which was the young Donne's fatal Cleopatra. It is a question of technique. The key to Donne's mature style is his use of logic: the more subtle and complex the emotion, the greater the logical pressure. The mature Donne organizes his poems in such a way that each shift of feeling seems to be substantiated logically. In the *Elegies*, however, the emotions are simpler and are sustained in their singleness. He adopts a stance and then develops it dramatically, not logically. So instead of a piece of elaborate human dialectics, he leaves you with a situation presented in the vivid coloring of a more or less single strong feeling.

Even the best of the *Elegies*, in fact, are more uncomplicatedly assertive than most of Donne's other work of the same standard. "Elegie IV. The Perfume", for instance, is perhaps the most inventive of all Donne's poems, but its wit is more ornamental than profound: it has gone into the puns, into the dramatic detail, into maintaining the overriding masculine independence. It is, in short, less analytic than energetic. The only deepening of tone comes at the moment when his masculinity itself is threatened:

> Onely, thou bitter sweet, whom I had laid
> Next mee, mee traiterously hast betraid . . .

It may seem odd that the perfume should inspire a couple
of lines which are as moving and as moved as anything
Donne ever wrote on the theme of the inconstant mistress.
But the reason comes a few lines later:

> By thee, the greatest staine to mans estate
> Falls on us, to be call'd effeminate . . .

The perfume, in fact, has undermined the whole basis of
this and most of the other *Elegies*. the almost belligerent
masculinity of the young Donne who was "a great visitor
of ladies."

The difference between the *Elegies* and Donne's maturest
technique is large and clear:

> *A nocturnall upon* S. Lucies *day,*
> *Being the shortest day.*

Tis the yeares midnight, and it is the dayes,
Lucies, who scarce seavcn houres herself unmaskes,
The Sunne is spent, and now his flasks
Send forth light squibs, no constant rayes;
    The worlds whole sap is sunke:
The generall balme th'hydroptique earth hath drunk,
Whither, as to the beds-feet, life is shrunke,
Dead and enterr'd; yet all these seeme to laugh,
Compar'd with mee, who am their Epitaph.

Study me then, you who shall lovers bee
At the next world, that is, at the next Spring:
    For I am every dead thing,
    In whom love wrought new Alchimie.
        For his art did expresse
A quintessence even from nothingnesse,
From dull privations, and leane emptinesse:
He ruin'd mee, and I am re-begot
Of absence, darknesse, death; things which are not.

All others, from all things, draw all that's good,
Life, soule, forme, spirit, whence they beeing have;
    I, by loves limbecke, am the grave
    Of all, that's nothing. Oft a flood
        Have wee two wept, and so
Drownd the whole world, us two; oft did we grow
To be two Chaosses, when we did show
Care to ought else; and often absences
Withdrew our soules, and made us carcasses.

But I am by her death, (which word wrongs her)
Of the first nothing, the Elixer grown;
   Were I a man, that I were one,
  I needs must know; I should preferre,
     If I were any beast,
Some ends, some means; Yea plants, yea stones detest,
And love; All, all some properties invest;
If I an ordinary nothing were,
As shadow, a light, and body must be here.

But I am None; nor will my Sunne renew.
You lovers, for whose sake, the lesser Sunne
   At this time to the Goat is runne
  To fetch new lust, and give it you,
     Enjoy your summer all;
Since shee enjoyes her long nights festivall,
Let mee prepare towards her, and let mee call
This houre her Vigill, and her Eve, since this
Both the yeares, and the dayes deep midnight is.

This is the only one of Donne's poems which might validly
be called "modern". As in *The Waste Land,* the poet is on
the rack to define a complex negative state which he apparently cannot fully understand and, what is even more perti-
nent to Donne's difficulty, which he cannot properly dra-
matize. The theme is a depression so deep as to verge on
annihilation (he wrote, after all, a defense of suicide). And
its root, I think, is inaction, or the impossibility of action,
as he described it in the famous letter to Goodyer:

> Therefore I would fain do something; but that I cannot
> tell what is no wonder. For to chuse, is to do: but to
> be no part of any body, is to be nothing.[2]

He tries to force some kind of clearing through this swad-
dling depression by bringing to bear upon it an extraordinarily tense logic and a great concentration of learning.
Each stanza moves forward to its own temporary resolution;
the twisted, pausing, in-turning movement clears to make way
for a direct but invariably negative statement:

> "The worlds whole sap is sunke";
> "Compar'd with mee, who am their Epitaph";
> "For I am every dead thing";
> "Things which are not";

[2] *Letters to Severall Persons of Honour,* 1651, p. 44.

"Made us carcasses";
"But I am none" (the resolution of the immensely
compressed previous stanza);

Unlike most of his other lyrics, the logic of "The Nocturnall" does not exorcise his troubles. Despite all the dialectic and the learning, despite the invocation of the outside lovers and even, in the third stanza, the invocation of
his own more dramatic love poems he is left with the blank
fact of his isolation. Yet although whatever pressure he
brings to bear on the situation produces no clear answer,
it does help him to achieve some kind of balance. The last
lines of the poem—"since this/Both the yeares, and the
dayes deep midnight is"—may simply be a restatement of
the first— "Tis the yeares midnight, and it is the dayes,
Lucies"—but they are a restatement with a difference: the
difficult, questioning movement of the start has been resolved into a clearer, more measured statement. He finishes,
that is, by *accepting* the depression, instead of trying, with
all the intellectual ingenuity at his command, to wriggle
through it. So the poem ends with his facing the adult ne-
cessity of living with grief and depression, instead of giving
in to them. Donne's logic and learning, in short, were the
prime forces in his emotional maturity *as a poet*.

It is the absence of this quality, incidentally, which marks
off Shakespeare's formal verse from Donne's:

They that have power to hurt and will do none,
That do not do the thing they most do show,
Who, moving others, are themselves as stone,
Unmoved, cold and to temptation slow,
They rightly do inherit heaven's graces
And husband nature's riches from expense;
They are the lords and owners of their faces,
Others but stewards of their excellence.
The summer's flow'r is to the summer sweet
Though to itself it only live and die,
But if that flow'r with base infection meet
The basest weed outbraves his dignity:
    For sweetest things turn sourest by their deeds;
    Lilies that fester smell far worse than weeds.

Like "The Nocturnall", Sonnet XCIV is also, in its way,
a rather modern poem: its mode is complex, negative and
founded perhaps on the same sexual anger and frustration
that produced Othello's "O thou weed/Who art so lovely

fair and smell'st so sweet/That the sense aches at thee, would thou hadst ne'er been born!" But unlike Donne's, Shakespeare's compression is all in the imagery rather than the argument. Where Donne often began with a straightforward situation (those famous, or infamous, dramatic openings) and then produced infinitely complicated arguments to justify it, Shakespeare begins with the abstractions and then gives them body. Even in the first two lines, of the Sonnet, the difficulty is more in the idea expressed than in the way it is expressed or in the distance suddenly travelled. Thereafter, the logic is emotional—from anger to a peculiarly savage irony to menace—and it proceeds by images. With Donne, on the other hand, strong emotion brings with it strong logic and a trick of twisting Aristotle and company to his own ends, almost as if he were trying to squeeze from them a kind of assurance.

However far, of course, Donne seems from the usual Elizabethan rhetoric, he did produce a rhetoric of his own. He produced it for his rare public performances—the two *Anniversaries,* for example—and it was the rhetoric of the intellectual, abstract and analytic. Hence, Ben Jonson's irritated declaration "That Dones Anniversarie was profane and full of Blasphemies. That he told Mr Done, if it had been written of ye Virgin Marie it had been something to which he answered that he described the Idea of a Woman and not as she was." In the *First Anniversarie* Donne dissects "the idea of a woman" in order to produce "An Anatomie of the World", a theological and political analysis of the state of corruption; that is, he was using the occasion to be deliberately less Donne the poet than Donne the learned wit, author of *Pseudo-Martyr.* The *Second Anniversarie,* "The Progresse of the Soule", is less abstract, more dramatic and, seemingly, more deeply felt. It is possible, indeed, that its roots were much more personal than those of the *First Anniversarie.* Donne apparently wrote it well before the date it was due, while he was staying with Sir Robert Drury in Amiens. He had gone abroad unwillingly, full of anxiety for his wife whom he left ill and pregnant. It was at Amiens that he had the terrible dream in which his wife appeared to him with a dead child in her arms.[3] It may be, then, that "the idea of a woman" was, in this instance, his wife, not Elizabeth Drury. Be that as it may, the dramatic meditation on death and the after-life is closer

[3] See R. C. Bald, *John Donne and the Drurys,* Cambridge, 1959. pp. 86-87, 89-90, 92-93.

to the style of Donne the preacher or Donne the author of the *Devotions* than to that of the more analytic theologian of the *First Anniversarie*. In both poems, his public personality is foremost. Their rhetoric is formally and formidably that of the intellectual, the debater.

Yet fundamentally it is the same rhetoric which, on less public occasions, is used to heighten a personal strength and richness. Philosophy, science, logic, divinity, poetry itself are all means to enhancing the dignity of the individual. His realism lies in the richness of the resources he brings to bear upon more or less conventional subjects and his ability never to falsify the full range of his response. Donne's achievement was to take a poetry over which the academic theorists were fiercely haggling, and break down the constrictions of mere aesthetic criteria; to take a dialectical form which had become rigid in centuries of scholastic wrangling, and break down its narrow casuistry; to take the sciences in all the imaginative strength of the new discoveries, and bring them all together as protagonists in the inward drama of his own powerful experience. He substantiated less a poetic technique than a form of intelligence which the most talented men of the following generation could use without, at any point, belying their natural gifts outside the realm of poetry. As a result, the style of Donne lasted until, under the imperative stresses of the Civil War, the whole mode of intelligence changed. We are now far enough removed from the tensions that split the seventeenth century to be able to judge Donne's monarchy of wit not as a trick or a fashion but as one of the greatest achievements of the poetic intelligence.

Chapter One

DONNE AND THE UNDERSTANDER

The statements was interesting but tough.
                                    'Huckleberry Finn'

THERE are two extraordinary things about the School of Donne. First, although it claims three exceptionally important and gifted poets—Donne, George Herbert and Marvell—and a higher standard of minor verse than any other school in English Literature, it seems to have been almost totally disregarded in its time. You can read through the sixteenth- and early seventeenth-century critical essays collected by Gregory Smith and Spingarn without realizing that there was any such thing as the School of Donne. The critical tradition descends from the Elizabethans to the Restoration seemingly without pause. It makes Donne's style seem an aberration.

Second, the minute amount of critical commentary that can be found—as distinct from personal tributes to the poets, which are legion—is all derogatory. The Metaphysicals are only mentioned in order to be knocked down contemptuously. And this, in some odd manner and for an odder reason, increased as the Metaphysicals became more and more things of the past. Merely by calling them 'Metaphysicals' their detractors dismissed them without reprieve. Even as late as 1921, Eliot, a trained metaphysician himself, commented: "The phrase has long done duty as a term of abuse, or as a label of a quaint and pleasant taste." The effect of this 'term of abuse' was itself unusual. There was almost no overt reaction against the School of Donne. The poets did not come in for that kind of attention at all. They were not dignified by discussion, disapproval or even detailed abuse, which is the usual procedure when a new school of writers replaces an old. They were simply ignored or dismissed absolutely as not being worth discussion.

These two omissions—no formal aesthetic and no critical discussion—sound very close, almost perhaps as though they

21

were one. They are not. The reasons why Donne, although very much an Elizabethan, was outside the Elizabethan poetic tradition are quite different from the reasons why the School of Donne—which was largely Caroline—was rejected so ignominiously within thirty-odd years of his death. The first may have helped the second, but that, really, is beside the point. My business in this first chapter will be to define what it was that separated Donne from the general Elizabethan practice. In the subsequent chapters I will discuss Donne's followers in terms of this definition. Finally, I will try to give some reasons why the Metaphysicals were so completely rejected at the Restoration.

It used to be the fashion to imagine that Donne's contemporaries couldn't, of course, understand him because he followed aesthetic theories too sophisticated for his time. For example, Cleanth Brooks once ended a definition of Metaphysical poetry: "The Metaphysical poet has confidence in the powers of the imagination. He is constantly remaking his world by relating into an organic whole the amorphous and heterogeneous and contradictory. Trusting in imaginative unity he refuses to depend upon non-imaginative classifications, those of logic and science." This is an odd statement: it might be remotely true of Eliot, though he would hardly encourage it; it is wholly true of Hart Crane and of late Mallarmé, and that was their misfortune. I can see, too, how one might explain some of the most striking effects of the Jacobean dramatists in this way. But it has nothing whatsoever to do with Donne. It is difficult, in fact, to see how anyone could have responded in this way to Donne's extraordinarily tough, dialectical verse.

For example, now we are over the shock of the conceit— the lovers as compasses, and the rest—it is remarkable how small a part, in cold blood, the device plays in Donne's verse. Dr Johnson may have been justified in making so much of it, but his subject was not Donne, it was Cowley. He also used Cleveland quite as much as he used the Master himself. And both were using Donne for their own ends. Donne himself was different. When in, say, 'Aire and Angels' he talks about his own progress in love—from the ideal to the overwhelmingly physical and back, finally, to a delicate harmony between the two—he bolsters his case by an elaborate argument from angelology. The logic is difficult and Grierson's notes are full of Latin quotations. Yet in this, as in those notorious compasses, there is no feeling at all that the poet is trying to bring off any violent, imaginative *coup*. The angels, the difficult metaphysical arguments about them and the presence of Aquinas behind the lot do not add up to a glowing and inexplicable poetic symbol in the manner of Baudelaire or Mallarmé. Instead, they are used to add dignity and importance to the human situation. The conceit, as such, is far less insisted upon than the logic; the tone of the piece is set by the steady repetition of small, argumentative copulas, like 'for', 'so', 'since', 'therefore', 'must be', 'then', and so forth, rather than the sudden and spectacular phrases like 'scattering bright'. What, in fact, is most remarkable in all Donne's work is not the surprisingness of the conceits but the fact that they do not jar at all with the general tenor of the poetry.

As a parenthesis, I should add that by refusing to treat Donne as though he were a Symbolist poet I am not coming down on the side of the Tuves. It is now a critical commonplace that although Renaissance criticism *can* be interpreted as wide enough and deep enough to include both Donne and Sidney or Spenser, the kind of poetry Donne wrote was utterly different from that of the traditional Elizabethans. Nor does Miss Tuve explain why there is no contemporary criticism of Donne, and precious little comment. This is a matter of the nature of Renaissance criticism: it was almost wholly theoretical; and the theories were largely derived from Italian and French and concerned with justifying English poets—thought to be a naïve and unskilled lot—by Italian and French practice. There was a little rhetorical analysis of verse, but there was no critical analysis at all. In fact, the only first-rate analytical critic the English Renaissance produced is Miss Rosemond Tuve. The critics of Donne's own time disregarded him because he disregarded, or at least was outside, their theories. And in England, outside the narrow path of prosody, criticism was theory. Obviously, a poet who responded with as much vitality as Donne to the intellectual tone of his time must have been perfectly aware of its poetic theories and conventions; but, for reasons I will try to give, they were not properly his business.

I have invoked the phrase 'intellectual tone' or its equivalent à propos of both the belligerently sixteenth-century and the belligerently twentieth-century ways of interpreting Donne. It is a crucial phrase. For one of the charms Donne holds for us is his difficulty; it goes with Eliot's maxim about poetry in our time having to be difficult. But difficulty was at least an issue, even if something less of a charm, in Donne's day. His friend Ben Jonson told Drummond "that

Donne . . . for not being understood would perish".[1] He did not mean, as some modern critics would argue, that Donne was aesthetically before his time and hence was bound, like Blake and all the other archetypal geniuses, to be misunderstood. In fact, it is hard to see quite what Jonson did mean, since every Renaissance poet worth his salt was supposed to be difficult. The idea is at least as old as the fourteenth century; Boccaccio makes great play with it in his *De Genealogia Deorum* (the relevant sections were probably written in the 1360's), and he in turn refers to the authority of Petrarch and St Augustine. That poetry was necessarily obscure was reaffirmed continually in Renaissance England, by, for instance, Harington, Sidney and Chapman; an exhaustive list would include most of the relatively traditional writers of poetics. Chapman deliberately 'darkened' Homer to put beyond dispute the poet's dignity and excellence.

But the Renaissance ideal was not a poetry which, like Donne's, was difficult in itself. Poetry was only difficult because it had to be, because its proper subject was itself difficult: that is, philosophy. Poetry, they thought, was a kind of sauce to make philosophy palatable to those with no particular taste for abstractions. Hence Sidney's statement:

> I say the Philosopher teacheth, but he teacheth obscurely, so as the learned onely can vnderstand him, that is to say, he teacheth them that are already taught; but the Poet is the food for the tenderest stomacks, the Poet is indeed the right Popular Philosopher, whereof *Esops* tales give good proof. . . .[2]

There was a telling example of this when a gentleman named Sir Lodowick Bryskett entreated Spenser:

> to instruct me in some hard points with which I cannot of myself understand . . . (and to declare) the great benefits which men obtaine by the knowledge of Morall Philosophie, and in making us to know what the same is, what be the parts thereof, whereby virtues are to be distinguished from vices; and finally that he will be pleased to run over in such order as he shall thinke

[1] *Conversations with William Drummond of Hawthornden*, 1619, *Ben Jonson*, ed. C. H. Herford and Percy Simpson, 11 vols., Oxford, 1925-1952, I, p. 138.

[2] Sir Philip Sidney, *A Defense of Poesie*, c. 1583, printed 1595; *Elizabethan Critical Essays*, ed. G. Gregory Smith, 2 vols., Oxford, 1904, I, p. 167.

good, such and so many principles and rules thereof as shall serve not only for my better instruction, but also for the contentment and satisfaction of you all ... (and he shall open) that goodly cabinet in which this excellent treasure of virtues lieth locked up from the vulgar sort.[3]

Spenser refused on the grounds that he had "already undertaken a work tending to the same effect ... under the title of a *Faerie Queene* to represent all the moral virtues". Of course, the *Faerie Queene* is obscure; no one has yet interpreted the thing satisfactorily. But it is not obscure because Spenser is thinking in any profound or original way. (Indeed, it may be obscure for precisely the opposite reason: because it is so muddled that he could hardly be considered to be thinking at all.) Such thinking as there is had been done beforehand by Plato, Aristotle, Plotinus, or, more probably, by such syncretic encyclopaedists as Ficino. Spenser's first function was that of the technician who, by varying his style with his subject as decorum required, 'put over' the ideas of the philosophers with as much invention and accomplishment as he could. He weaved, as they put it, profit to pleasure, and so justified his art pragmatically. As his contemporary, Sir John Harington, has it, using Sidney's metaphor:

> The weaker capacities will feede themselves with the pleasantness of the historie and the sweetness of the verse, some that have stronger stomackes will as it were take a further taste of the Morall sence, a third sort, more high conceited then they, will digest the Allegorie.[4]

The business of the professional poet was to cater in an improving way for as large a public as he could. In doing so he was as subordinate to the moral truths of the philosophers as he was dependent on his patron.

Harington's third and highest conceited class of readers was called 'The Understanders'. Continually, at the end of the sixteenth century and until at least the middle of the seventeenth, more ambitious literature had always some preface or admonishment to these Understanders. So did Donne's poems when they finally appeared two years after his death. But there is a radical difference in what was ex-

[3] Sir Lodowick Bryskett, *A Discourse of Civil Life*, 1600, quoted by H. S. V. Jones, *A Spenser Handbook*, New York, 1930, pp. 30-1.

[4] Sir John Harington, *A Brief Apologie of Poetrie*, 1591; Gregory Smith, II, pp. 203-4.

pected of the ideal Understander of Spenser and of Donne.

It is a question, quite simply, of the poet's authority; a question of the relationship between the poet and his reader, and between the poet and his material. Boccaccio advised the mediaeval reader:

> I repeat my advice to those who would appreciate poetry, and unwind its difficult involutions. You must read, you must persevere, you must sit up nights, you must inquire and exert the utmost power of your mind. If one way does not lead to the desired meaning, take another; if obstacles arise, then still another; until, if your strength holds out, you will find that clear which at first looked dark. For we are forbidden by divine command to give that which is holy to dogs, or to cast pearl before swine.[5]

This sounds very like a mid-seventeenth century university wit struggling with the verse of one of the last and most decadent Metaphysicals, Samuel Austin, a poor imitator of Cleveland:

> I read a Verse of thine, then make a halt,
> (For though I *taste* it not, I'm sure ther's Salt:)
> And study for the meaning; and am vext;
> I finde; cry *eureka:* and read the next.
> It is (let none for *Recreation* look)
> *A very study t'understand thy Book.*[6]

But there is a difference. It lies in Boccaccio's phrase 'the desired meaning'. This is a motion towards a larger context of moral purpose. The duty of the Christian poet is to teach by delight; his work is accommodated to religious purposes which transcend his own. It is 'holy' and 'proceeds', Boccaccio says a little earlier, 'from the bosom of God'. That a poem should exist on a number of levels at once was, so to speak, its God-given justification. Even the rationalist Bacon indulged in the game of allegorical interpretation of the classics, converting myth into parable.[7] On the other hand, W. P.'s problem is not to discover a meaning that is hidden, inner and mystical, not to give poetry ultimate justification;

---

[5] *Boccaccio on Poetry*, being the Preface and the XIV and XV Books of Boccaccio's *Genealogia Deorum Gentilium*, translated by Charles G. Osgood, Princeton, 1930, p. 62.

[6] *Naps Upon Parnassus*, 1658. '*Incerti Authoris*', by W. P. . . . A4.

[7] See Charles William Lemmi, *The Classic Deities in Bacon*, Baltimore, 1933.

it is to make immediate sense of the lines. He is not puzzling out a Christian interpretation, he wants the poet's meaning. When he studies 't'understand' (the usual word), his problem is to unravel the syntax and allusion. The frame of reference, the wrenching of the style, the learning, are all the poet's own. In short, the traditional Renaissance poet, as a teacher and technician, seeks a large, moving impersonality; the Metaphysical, as a wit, demands intellectual agility and personal response. Austin's strong lines were something of a joke, his obscurity a tasteless parody of the real thing. But they were not eccentric; on the contrary, they were a clumsy attempt to be fashionable. The *Elegies* on Donne are full of tributes to the difficulty of his work:

> Indeed so farre above its Reader, good,
> That wee are thought wits, when 'tis understood.

That, the most cogent, is by Jasper Mayne. He has travelled a great distance from the idea that poetry should delight and instruct the reader. Instead, it is as though Donne's poetry were a test of the reader's capabilities. It is, certainly, the latter's intellectual worth that is in question, not that of the poet. Donne produced his own standards of wit. Instead of serving philosophy, he used it. For example, the end of 'The Good-morrow':

> What ever dyes, was not mixt equally;
> If our two loves be one, or, thou and I
> Love so alike, that none doe slacken, none can die.

Grierson's notes on this have a quotation from Aquinas and a summary of the scholastic doctrine of the soul. Behind them, I suppose, looms Aristotle. But there are two things to note: first, that there is absolutely no sense of surprise or disproportion in bringing the philosophers in to a love poem. Second, Donne is not interested in Aquinas's or Aristotle's ideas *for themselves;* he is merely using them to give weight to his own arguments. His interest is in his personal situation, not in the philosophers. They merely add a certain serious grandeur to Donne's feelings. Compare that with an excellent passage like the 'Garden of Adonis' in *The Faerie Queene.* Spenser is elaborately and beautifully illustrating the philosophers; they are his subject, his verse their accessory. Ideas for Spenser were separate entities, like idols he could walk round, peer at and make obeisance to. For Donne they were pillars more or less useful in supporting his own building. The reader was supposed to recognize them without any help from the poet. This is why he announced early in his career, in the preface to *The Progresse of the Soule*, "I will have no such readers as I can teach".

The difference between that and the accepted idea of the poet as 'the right popular philosopher', as Sidney called him, is obvious. But I can't believe that by disclaiming any interest in ill-equipped readers, or by calling *The Progresse of the Soule*

> this sullen Writ,
> Which just so much courts thee, as thou dost it

Donne was revealing, as Arnold Stein once suggested, a stoical avoidance of popularity.[8] It was, instead, a strong way of saying that he was not a professional poet. And this is the essential difference between Donne and the other Elizabethans. It meant that he could go his own way without the constriction of the poetical theories and theoretical duties to the public. Donne was not a professional poet. Instead, he was trained as a lawyer; he became the personal secretary and friend of Lord Ellesmere, the Lord Chancellor of England, who made him an M.P.; he was the writer of a learned book of political theology, *Pseudo-Martyr;* and he finished as the most eminent divine of his day. He was, in fact, a wit, which meant, distinctly, 'a man of intellect'.

He was, moreover, a wit writing for wits. For example, he sent some poems to Sir Henry Goodyer for him to pass on to the Countess of Bedford, one of the most renowned patronesses of the time. In the letter that went with them he said: "but (I) intreat you by your friendship, that by this occasion of versifying, I be not traduced, nor esteemed light in that Tribe, and that house where I have lived".[9] This is just one of a large number of comments, scattered through the letters, where Donne emphasized that he was something more than a mere poet. The 'tribe', his circle, esteemed him as one of the most accomplished and gifted men of his day; as such, his verse was *almost* a failure of seriousness. Consequently, his letters steadily decry his reputation as a poet, which he seems to have considered as something trivial and to one

---

[8] 'Donne's Obscurity and the Elizabethan Tradition', *English Literary History*, XIII, 1946, pp. 98-118.

[9] *Letters to Severall Persons of Honour*, 1651, p. 104.

side of his real accomplishments. It was only later when, as the greatest preacher of his time, he was beyond poetry, that he had, in some of the sermons, a good word to say for the art.

Not only Donne's letters, but his poetry too, are full of side-swipes at the whining, undignified triviality of verse. Of course, it was ironical to denigrate poetry in the very process of writing it so magnificently. But Donne's attacks were all made from a single stronghold: a distaste for the fevered unreality of poetic conventions. Comments like:

> Love's not so pure, and abstract, as they use
> To say, which have no Mistresse but their Muse
> ('Loves growth')

or

> It was a theame
> For reason, much too strong for phantasie
> ('The Dreame')

are made in the same spirit as Plato's irritated banishment of the poets from his republic, or as Bacon's similar dismissal:

> Poetry is as a dream of learning; and a thing sweet and varied, and that would be thought to have in it something divine; a character which dreams likewise affect. But now it is time for me to awake, and rising above the earth, to wing my way through the clear air of Philosophy and Sciences.[10]

Though the kind of intellectual discipline Bacon stood for was ultimately turned against the School of Donne—that is the theme of my last chapter—they are very close in their initial impulse: an irritated desire to have done with posturing and to talk sense. Professor Morris Croll has written that

> Aristotelianism, mediaeval scholasticism, Bartholism, Platonism, Ciceronianism, Euphuism, and whatever other shadowy phantoms of reality had haunted the Renaissance, had already been severally exposed to the criticism of reason. But Bacon gathered them all to-

[10] *De Augmentis*, III, i; *Works of Sir Francis Bacon*, ed. James Spedding, R. L. Ellis and D. D. Heath, 1857-59. 7 vols., IV, p. 336.

gether within the limits of a single survey, and covered them all over with one narrow *hic jacet*.[11]

One can parallel this, vice for vice, in Carew's *Elegie* on Donne. In short, scattered through Donne's poems are his own poetic equivalents of Bacon's three abuses of learning: *fantastical learning,* or exaggeration and rhetorical extravagance; *contentious learning,* or poetic jealousy and 'Satyrique thornes'; *delicate learning,* or the posturing unrealities of Platonic love.

Donne reacted against the pretensions in the name of common sense and intellectual standards, never in the name of poetic principles. The continual impression his poems make is of the mind in action, its resources insisted upon, even in the teeth of technique. Miss Helen Gardner has pointed out that the nearest Donne ever got to a theory of poetry is in this passage from the sermons:

> In all Metrical compositions . . . the force of the whole piece is for the most part left to the shutting; the whole frame of the Poem is a beating out of a piece of gold, but the last clause is as the impression of the stamp, and that is it that makes it currant.[12]

For Donne, the beating out was, as often as not, a careful and exact progression of argument; the stamping, the application of the image and the final clinching twist of the dialectic. The dialectic, in fact, is the controlling principle. Miss Tuve once said that the difference between Elizabethan and Metaphysical conceits is in the complexity of the logical parallels they pursue,[13] and the kind of detailed study that has been made of the logic of Donne's poetry [14] shows that he respected the rules of logic far more than those of current poetics. Both Donne's intelligence and his images are, in fact, more rational than fantastical. This was precisely the implication of Carew's tribute to Donne's preaching:

[11] Morris W. Croll, 'Attic Prose: Lipsius, Montaigne and Bacon', *Schelling Anniversary Papers*, N.Y., 1923, pp. 117-50. See also, 'Muret and the History of "Attic" Prose', *Publications of the Modern Language Association of America*, XXXIX, 1924, pp. 254-309, and ' "Attic" Prose in the Seventeenth Century', *Studies in Philology*, XVIII, 1921, pp. 79-128.

[12] Sermon LV, *LXXX Sermons*, 1640, p. 549, quoted in *The Metaphysical Poets*, ed. Helen Gardner, 1957, p. 21.

[13] *Elizabethan and Metaphysical Imagery*, Chicago, 1947, p. 294.

[14] For example, by Miss E. L. Wiggins, 'Logic in the Poetry of John Donne', *Studies in Philology*, XLII, 1945, pp. 41-60.

And the deepe knowledge of dark truths so teach,
As sense might judge, what phansie could not reach.

This has nothing to do with the sensuous apprehension of thought, and everything to do with the reason. 'Sense' here means 'intellect'. Donne's Monarchy of Wit extended beyond that of 'phansie' (imagination), the conventional realm of the poet; [15] it was of reason, of the understanding.

I suggest Donne himself emphasized this so determinedly in order to make clear his distance from the common, professional poets. Ben Jonson told Drummond that "Done said to him he wrott that Epitaph on Prince Henry . . . to match Sir Edward Herbert in obscurenesse".[16] But perhaps he also wrote it in that exceptionally crabbed, obscure style because it was one of his rare poems to appear publicly in a printed book: it was published, along with contributions from a number of his group, in Joshua Sylvester's *Lachrymae Lachrymarum* in 1613. In the same way, although Donne in his love songs can be as mellifluous and easy as the best of the Elizabethans, he never wrote in that way when it seemed most expected of him. Some of his most difficult poems are the verse-letters to important ladies like the Countesses of Bedford and Huntingdon and Mrs Magdalen Herbert, whom he was anxious to impress with his powers of wit.

It is the same with Donne's notorious metrical harshness. The few comments his contemporaries passed on his style make it sound as though to be a Metaphysical poet all that was necessary was to ignore metrical rules. But just as Donne made no effort to cajole his audience by writing easily, or on palatable and improving subjects, nor by paying court to what were considered the 'poetic' feelings, so he made no attempt to please anyone by his 'smoothness of numbers', or by any great display of technique. He deliberately wrote his early satires harshly, partly because that was how satires were supposed to be written (no one imagined that they were designed to please), and partly to disclaim any particular interest in the craft of poetry. And he did this at a period when the professionals were quarrelling fiercely about the nature of English metre. Donne's metrical harshness, then, like his obscurity, was a way of hanging out his sign. It read: 'Wits and Amateurs Only'.

This, in itself, was nothing very revolutionary. There were

15 "The lunatic, the lover and the poet **Are** of imagination all compact." *Midsummer Night's Dream*, V, i.

16 *Loc. cit.* I, p. 136.

a number of writers trying to free their styles from the smooth falsities of Renaissance rhetoric, but the rest were working in prose: Lipsius and Muret in Latin, Montaigne in French and Bacon in English and Latin. These were the masters of what Croll called the 'Attic' style. Obviously, Donne was naturally sympathetic to the style: it was the *genus humile*, which was the style of philosophical discourse; it fostered logical brevity and what was called 'significant darkness'; according to Lipsius, "Everything is said for the sake of the argument". In short, the 'Attic' style employed 'figures of wit' rather than the 'figures of sound' of Ciceronian rhetoric. All these were qualities which Donne continually emphasized in his own work. So perhaps the kind of thing he was trying to do may have been made easier by the fact that the 'Attic' style was already there, even though not in English. But it did not exist as a ready-made set of devices. It was far more a matter of avoiding tricks and contortions of style. And this, again, fitted flush with Donne's distaste for the poetical.

The most important common principle in the 'Attic' writers was, however, this: rhetoric was formal, public and self-conscious, and its devices were designed to cajole the listeners into attention; hence to abandon rhetoric, the art of public speaking, was to abandon, in principle, the art of public pleasing. They replaced formality by personal sincerity and wrote in a deliberately off-hand manner for the pleasure of their intimate friends. Montaigne is quite open about this in his essay on letter writing; it is behind Donne's comments on *The Progresse of the Soule* and the continual stream of remarks he made in verse-letters to friends about his harshness. It is as though he were always congratulating himself on writing badly. Not to bother about one's metre was a token of intimacy. And this intimacy was no less because Donne's work was well known in his own day. With two or three exceptions, he published none of it. Like the earlier Tudor Court poets, he circulated his poems in manuscript among some of his friends,[17] and those who were lucky enough to get hold of the poems made copies for their friends, who in turn made copies for their friends, and so on. That is why so many manuscripts of Donne's poems have survived. Nevertheless, the *original* circle of Donne's readers was very select.

So far we have established that the audience of Donne's poetry was different from that of the run of Elizabethan

[17] See J. W. Saunders, 'The Stigma of Print', *Essays in Criticism*, 1951, I, pp. 139-64.

verse; they came to his poetry fully equipped, not having, or wanting, to be taught obliquely by delight. On the contrary, since Donne's technique, or his avoidance of technique, was itself a token of intimacy, his way of constantly bringing to bear on personal subjects the full force of his great learning may well have been another way of closing the circle. The implication is, of course, that his friends did not want to be taught or in any way condescended to; they were perfectly able to keep up with his arguments and his mass of half-references to a great range of subjects.

This means that, by the canons of professional Elizabethan poetry, Donne wrote in a specialized way which would not have been generally familiar, possibly not even acceptable to, the wider audience of published poetry. And he wrote this way not merely because this was the way his sensibility worked but because this was the expression of the taste and sensibility of a whole group, his circle. In his middle age Donne sent to a friend, Sir Robert Ker, a copy of a controversial prose work of his, *Biathanatos*. In the letter that went with it he remarked that "no hand hath passed upon it to copy it, nor many eyes to read it: onely to some particular friends in both Universities, then when I writ it, I did communicate it." [18] This, I think, was what happened originally to the poems. The questions are, then, who were Donne's particular friends, and what was it that made them so eager to read poetry which was not only very difficult but which wantonly disregarded the theorists of Elizabethan literature? Were they modern poets with an elaborately experimental aesthetic, but born three and a quarter centuries before their time? Or were they, like our angry young men, in deliberate revolt against the orthodox establishment?

They were neither. They may not have formed the poetic establishment—which was made up of professional poets, patronized by aristocrats and justified by Continental theories—but they were essentially of the Establishment in the other sense: that is, of the influential ruling classes. It was their preoccupation with being precisely this that gave their poetry its distinctive taste.

When I speak of Donne's circle I mean his earlier group of friends; for, according to Izaak Walton, his biographer, and Ben Jonson, his friend, Donne wrote most of his verse when he was in his early twenties. So his most important and formative audience was the circle of friends he had before his marriage in 1601. It is, of course, impossible to be

[18] *Letters to Severall Persons of Honour*, 1651, p. 19.

definite about who was Donne's friend and who was not, but it is not hard to find out who were the nucleus of his group. These are the men to whom he wrote letters or poems, who wrote or dedicated works to him, or who are associated with him by Walton or in contemporary memoirs, literary fragments, and so on.

In order, then, to show what kind of person Donne was writing for, what interests and tone they might have had in common, here is a list of fifteen men who were his friends when he was writing his early poems. All that is needed for the moment is to give their names and say what later became of them. There was Sir Henry Wotton, poet, later Ambassador to Venice and finally Provost of Eton; John Hoskyns, M.P., Judge, Sergeaunt-at-Law, poet and author of one of the few good pieces of Elizabethan criticism, *Directions for Speech and Style;* Sir Richard Baker, M.P. and High Sheriff of Oxfordshire, historian, essayist and translator; Christopher Brook who became a leading lawyer and acquired a considerable—and quite unmerited—reputation as a poet; his brother Samuel Brook, the officiator at Donne's secret marriage, who was also a minor poet and even a dramatist (though in Latin), and finished as the Royal Chaplain, Professor of Divinity at Gresham College and Master of Trinity; Rowland Woodward, a minor diplomat and courtier; his kinsman, Thomas Woodward, a fairly distinguished lawyer; Beaupré Bell, son of the Chief Baron of the Exchequer; Everard Gilpin, the satirist; Sir John Roe, poet and soldier; Sir William Cornwallis, politician and first English imitator of Montaigne; Sir Robert Cotton, the antiquary; Sir Francis Wooley, who put up the Donnes during the difficult years of their disgrace; Sir Tobie Mathew, an intimate friend of Bacon, a diplomat and *belle lettriste;* and, finally, there was Donne's closest friend, Sir Henry Goodyer, soldier, courtier and patron of the arts.[19]

It was a talented and varied group, the members of which had at least four things in common: first, they all went through the same educational mill as Donne, at Oxford or Cambridge, and then at the Inns of Court; second, they all entered the most respected professions—diplomacy, law, politics, the Church, or, at worst, the army—or they took up administrative positions at court; third, none of them was born into the powerful aristocracy; most of them, like Donne, came from the wealthy middle classes or landed gentry; if they were knighted, as many of them were, they were

19 See Appendix I.

knighted more for their services than their birth; lastly, nearly every one wrote poetry of a kind, but only one actually published at all seriously: that was Gilpin, and he plagiarized Donne in order to do so.

In short, Donne's first and most formative audience was made up of the young, literary, middle-class intellectual élite who, like Donne himself, were to become the leading professional men of the time.[20] This, in Carew's words, was "The Universall Monarchy of Wit", men of intellect and wide, varied talents, who like the subjects in any other monarchy, had language, customs, conventions and interests in common. Donne was their "King, that rul'd as hee thought fit". But that merely meant he was more powerful, more authoritative than the rest. He was not apart from them. Instead, he was apart from the professional poets. The only one who could claim him as a friend was Ben Jonson and he, who was also one of the few poets properly accepted as an equal by all the wits, submitted his verse to Donne's criticism and spoke of him—except in his private conversations with Drummond—with an unusual deference. For the rest, Donne had nothing to do with the literary world. When he was attacked—as he was obliquely at times—he did not reply; when he was invited to appear in anthologies, with two exceptions, both 'witty' collections, he refused.[21]

After most of the names in the list above I have put 'poet'. The crux of the matter is, then, the kind of work they turned out. For none of them are known as Metaphysical poets in the current sense of that term. The School of Donne, such as it was, came later. So if the members of the original circle were all writing pleasant, traditional Elizabethan verse, it would be difficult to understand Donne's originality; he really would appear as something of a phoenix. But, a couple of them excepted, they were not. When poems by Donne's circle have been published, they have mostly been ascribed by early editors to Donne himself. They look, most of them, like his worst apprentice works: they are harsh and colloquial—which in this instance means wholly unmetrical—their wit is entirely dialectical, argumentative and often obscure, with sliding half-references to the philosophers and authorities. Relatively, their work is free of what we now

---

[20] Mr. I. A. Shapiro has shown that later in his life, when Donne attended the feasts at the Mermaid, the company was made up of precisely the same kind of people, though richer and more firmly established. See 'The "Mermaid Club" ', *Modern Language Review*, XIV, 1950, pp. 6-17.

[21] See Appendix II.

think of as Metaphysical conceits. The one thing they all insist on—in much the same way as modern poets have made a cult of the image—is their harshness. It was as though the one way of showing that one was a member of the circle was, as Ben Jonson suggested in *Timber*, to write badly:

> *Others*, that in composition are nothing, but what is rough, and broken. . . . And if it would come gently, they trouble it of purpose. They would not have it run without rubs, as if that stile were more strong and manly, that stroke the eare with a kind of uneven(n)esse. These men erre not by chance, but knowingly, and willingly; they are like men that affect a fashion by themselves, have some singularity in a Ruffe, Cloake, or Hat-band; or their beards, specially cut to provoke beholders, and set a marke upon themselves. They would be reprehended, while they are look'd on. And this vice, one that is in authority with the rest, loving, delivers over to them to bee imitated: so that oft-times the faults which he fell into, the others seeke for: This is the danger, when vice becomes a *Precedent*.[22]

Of course, carelessness about the niceties of style was, by 'Attic' canons, both a mark of intimacy and also a sign that one was concentrating on *what* one was saying, not on *how* —which is a traditional Ciceronian distinction between the genders of style. As Benlowes, one of the most extreme of the Metaphysicals, put it: "The masculine and refined pleasures of the understanding transcend the feminine and sensual of the eye".[23]

If, then, Donne ruled over 'the Monarchy of Wit', and if the qualities his subjects valued most were his intimacy of tone, ease of learning and dialectic, then Donne for his circle was not obscure. They had too much in common, they used the same shorthand. Obviously, none of his circle was on the same level as Donne, but he was never as remote from them as he was from the run of Elizabethan poetasters. The pleasure they got from his and from each other's poetry was the same kind of enjoyment that one of the circle, Sir Richard Baker, found in Tacitus:

[22] *Timber, Or Discoveries*, 1641; *Ben Jonson*, ed. C. H. Herford, Percy and Evelyn Simpson, 11 vols., Oxford, 1925-47, VIII, p. 585.

[23] Preface to *Theophila*, 1652. *Minor Poets of the Caroline Period*, ed. George Saintsbury, 3 vols., Oxford, 1905, I, p. 319.

(His) very obscurity is pleasing to whosoever by labouring about it, findes out the true meaning; for then he
counts it an issue of his own braine, and taking occasion from these sentences, to goe further than the
thing he reads, and that without being deceived, he takes
the like pleasure as men are wont to take from hearing
metaphors, finding the meaning of him that useth them.[24]

It was the coterie pleasure of recognizing one another's wit,
almost as though the readers were let in on a secret. The
style presumed on the fact that both poets and audience had
had the same kind of training, done much the same
reading and shared the same taste for the sceptical, paradoxical and, above all, the dialectical.

This was very different from the moral, craftsmanly,
theoretical emphasis of the Spenser-Sidney-Fulke-Greville
circle. But obviously neither that nor the kind of coterie
shorthand I have described was any short-cut to major poetry.
Rather the contrary. That presumably is why Jonson said
"That Donne , . for not being understood, would perish",
and why extreme coterie writers, like Cleveland and Benlowes, have perished, except for scholars' occasional and
mildly eccentric curiosity. But Donne and his coterie, though
Anti-Petrarchan, were not in strict formal opposition to anyone else's aesthetics, for the good reason that their main
interests were not in technical matters. Their literariness was
merely one side of their culture. The advantage of this for
Donne was not that the group put pressure on him to write
in a particular way but that they relieved him of the pressure to use a certain style and acknowledge certain pieties.

The test of Donne's genius is that, unlike the other
members of his circle, he was able to use this freedom.
Even his contemporaries granted that he was one of the
most original poets in the language; Carew founded his
elegy on this idea and Ben Jonson called him "the first poet
in the world in some things"—which could mean first in
time as well as in quality. Neither of them meant that he
abandoned so many of the poetic conventions of his time in
quest of, say, a kind of Expressionism or experimentalism.
He was, after all, a great master of the accepted lyric modes
and wrote a number of poems clearly intended for music. But
he modified what was there to his own ends.

[24] Sir Richard Baker, Preface to his translation of Malvezzi's
Discourses upon Cornelius Tacitus, 1642; quoted by Roy Daniells,
'English Baroque and Deliberate Obscurity', *Journal of Aesthetics*, V,
1948, p. 119.

Donne's originality was not a matter of the outer forms of his verse, nor of the trick of the conceit, but of what he did to the language of poetry. Fundamentally, he merely adapted it to his own voice, but this was not a voice that had, as such, spoken before in poetry. In the most vital sense of an abused term, it was the voice of the intellectual. When, for example, Eliot said, "A thought to Donne was an experience; it modified his sensibility", he was, in a way, no more than glossing Donne's own description of himself: "I was diverted by the worst voluptuousnes, which is an Hydroptique immoderate desire of humane learning and language".[25] Donne was an intellectual not because he paraded ideas, but because ideas, learning, dialectic and tough, sceptical rationality were *emotionally important* to him. And so when they appeared in his poetry in support of a peculiarly personal argument in a peculiarly personal situation, they seemed natural and inevitable. So they appeared without any change of manner. They were part of the subtle checks and pressures and flow of that intelligent but sometimes slightly off-hand speaking voice in which Donne dealt with every subject, no matter how nominally imposing. So his poems are at once extremely complex and, because complexity of reference and mood is inevitable in intelligent talk, extremely simple.

Other Elizabethan poets were colloquial, but always in a slightly formal way. When Sidney writes:

"Fool", said my Muse to me, "look in thy heart and write"

he makes you realize that he is choosing the simple colloquial style for a specific rhetorical effect. Donne is simple without that air of formal device. He is, instead, so much on top of his complex material that he can deal with it directly, without needing formal devices. Similarly, when intellectual matters had appeared in verse before Donne, they were always something apart. Either they were authorities towards whom the poet made obeisance, or, in order to become 'poetic', they were personified, made into allegory. In either event, they appeared always as something else and were always a little beyond the poet. They never impinged on the living centre of his work. And this meant that poetry itself was something essentially apart and dealt only with a specialized kind of life.

[25] *Letters to Severall Persons of Honour*, 1651, p. 50.

The difference between this and Donne's work is in the latter's wholeness. It might perhaps be called, in Eliot's words, the work of 'the unified sensibility'; I prefer the term 'realism'. Donne is the first intellectual realist in English poetry. This realism came about partly, I think, because Donne found the conventional poetical attitudes tiresome, partly because he was sympathetic to the strong anti-rhetorical movement of the time, and partly because he was professionally committed to other intellectual disciplines unrelated to poetry, to manage which nothing less than analytical intelligence and a sense of fact would do. All this complexity, in fact, was *natural* to him, it was not part of an adopted style or a formally adopted topic. So it appeared as part of his direct personal responses. This realism altered the language of poetry because for the first time a writer was dealing in compelling poetic terms with the intellectual adult's full experience in all its immediacy.

This, I think, answers two of the questions I put at the beginning. First, the School of Donne contains the best minor poetry in the language because it required a great deal of intelligence and training and adult understanding to be able to write in that style at all. It could only come from intelligent, educated men, at their most intelligent, with their learning worn easily and writing with a colloquial sense of reality, though in all seriousness and conviction, and without censoring any areas of their sensibility. "To write on their plan", said Dr Johnson, "it was at least necessary to read and think." Second, the more orthodox poets were able successfully to ignore Donne and his School because the kind of intelligence the Metaphysicals used was the least exclusively 'poetical' in the language. Their poetry belonged to the busier, tougher, waking world of professional men, rather than to the glowing, specialized and remote world of the exclusively poetical.

Consider, for example, Spenser and Donne both writing formal poems for marriages. When Spenser writes:

Sweet Thames, run softly, till I end my song

he is talking not about the marriage, nor about its setting, but about his art; it is his *song* that is to *run softly* and *sweet*. But when Donne writes:

To night put on perfection, and a womans name

he is talking about the whole process of marriage and

39

maturity. He is, I am told, using a truism from Aristotle to do so. But he is so little self-conscious about the reference and is using it so thoroughly for his own ends that it appears in the poem not as some grand and immutable piece of wisdom but as a truth that he has arrived at, as the bride is about to, through his own feelings.

Perhaps, then, I might re-word Dr Johnson's praise of the Metaphysicals: not "To write on their plan it was at least necessary to read and think", but "To write on Donne's plan it was at least necessary to live and think; to write on Spenser's, to read and to write".

Chapter Two

THE STYLE AND THE COURTIERS

I

IN GRIERSON's classic anthology of Metaphysical poetry there are only two of Donne's immediate contemporaries represented: John Hoskyns and Sir Henry Wotton. And they are there more, presumably, out of piety than for any particularly Metaphysical poetry they wrote. Though the Metaphysicals were a more varied band than usually acknowledged, they were all at least a generation younger than Donne. Hence the better name for them is the School of Donne, for none could have written their own best work without him. At their most distinctive they borrowed little from him directly, yet they relied heavily on the new idiom he had created. They depended on him as settlers depend on a pioneer. Many of them knew him, but he was, to nearly all, an older man. This slight disparity in age meant that they were more able than his exact contemporaries to recognize his originality critically. Because he was personally no longer quite one of them, voicing their exact interests, quirks and enthusiasms, they understood his poems better as poems. They were open to the full effect of recognition and establishment: that personal respect and critical distance which combine to make a poetic influence. Hence one of the best pieces of critical writing on Donne is also a personal tribute: Carew's *Elegie*.

I have been trying to suggest that the most important influence Donne exerted on English poetry has little to do with the technical trick of the conceit and a great deal to do with intellectual tone. He changed the pressure of informal intelligence on verse. And so, however well his followers understood his work critically, they were also, directly or obliquely, influenced by him personally. Even if they did not actually know him, they knew and admired his kind of intelligence. For Donne was clearly one of those writers, like Ben Jonson and Dr Johnson, Blake and Lawrence, whose importance as a poet is closely linked to his vitality as a person. Even at the Restoration, when Donne was rejected as a poet, he was still admired as a great figure: Dryden granted him that when he wrote "I may safely say of this present age, that if we are not so great wits as Donne, yet certainly we are better poets".

Many of the poets in Grierson's anthology had come under the immediate impact of that wit. A good number must have heard him preach, a few knew him personally, and they, in turn, were closely connected with other members of the school. The main channel of his influence was the Herbert family. The two sons of Donne's friend Magdalen Herbert were both deeply in debt to his poetry and both were friends of other writers supported in the same way. Edward, Lord Herbert of Cherbury, knew Donne well: Donne wrote him letters, one of them in verse, and presented him with a copy of *Biathanatos*, flatteringly inscribed. Herbert, for his part, took Aurelian Townshend to France as his companion, in 1608-09; Carew was his secretary when he returned to Paris in 1619; all three exchanged verses. Carew, in turn, was a friend of Suckling, Davenant and Godolphin and, since they coincided at Court, he probably knew Lovelace. The latter certainly knew Marvell, who wrote a commendatory poem to *Lucasta* (1649). George Herbert, Edward's brother, was at Westminster with Henry King, who had been Prebendary of St Paul's shortly before Donne became its Dean. Both he and Herbert received copies of the seal which Donne, according to Walton, sent to 'his dearest friends'. It was, nominally, by following Herbert's example that Vaughan and Crashaw were gathered into the Metaphysical fold. Crashaw was a good friend of Cowley. Both probably knew Cleveland. And so on.

Nothing particularly conclusive, of course, can be shown by this House-that-Jack-built method of association. The only reason for indulging in it at all is to show that the School of Donne, like his original circle, was fairly close knit. It was more a School than a haphazard grouping of individuals. All its members were amateurs, few published when they were alive and, in their three categories, they could all assume a close community of taste and background. These categories are, admittedly, arbitrary, but the term 'Metaphysical Poets' seems to me to cover three rather different styles, or at least three different uses of Donne's poetic discoveries. Roughly, they correspond to the divisions in Grierson's anthology: there are the Love Poems, or the style of the courtiers; the Divine Poems, which is not the style of divinity or theology but of the poetry of religious experience; finally, there is what Grierson calls Miscellanies—in other words, the style of the University men.

The Metaphysical style, like any other large and imposing object, either disappears when you try to look at it too closely, or it grows until it fills the whole picture. I have resisted the temptation to claim as Metaphysical all the poems of the period which I most like. For example, if you stand back a little from the picture it is impossible to include Herrick's masterpiece, 'A Nuptiall Song, or Epithalamie, on Sir *Clipsoby Crew* and his Lady'. Yet it has what was once the chief requirement of a Metaphysical poem: it is peculiarly modern. It has some extraordinary rhythmical innovations which make it sound, at one point, more like Hopkins than Herrick:

> On then, and though you slow-
> ly go, yet, howsoever, go.

In two other places the poet seems to be encroaching on ground that has since been more carefully worked over:

> 'tis we,
> Who count this night as long as three,
> Lying alone,
> Telling the Clock strike Ten, Eleven, Twelve, One.

might have been written by W. H. Auden. Whilst the climax of the poem:

> And to your more bewitching, see, the proud
> Plumpe Bed beare up, and swelling like a cloud,
> Tempting the two too modest; can
> Yee see it brusle like a Swan,
> And you be cold
> To meet it, when it woo's and seemes to fold
> The Armes to hugge it? throw, throw
> Your selves into the mighty over-flow
> Of that white Pride, and Drowne
> The night, with you, in floods of Downe.

rises to a pitch of imaginative excitement which makes the poet wrench the language until it sounds, as W. W. Robson has remarked, like Mallarmé:

> Cet unanime blanc conflit
> D'une guirlande avec la même,
> Enfui contre la vitre blême
> Flotte plus qu'il n'ensévelit.

But modern or not, the sustained personal gusto of the poem owes almost nothing to Donne and very little to Ben Jonson. It makes the work simply the most original and imaginative that Herrick ever wrote—predictable, perhaps, from the striking, though sometimes rather calculated cleverness of some of his other poems, but not expected.

There is, however, a moment in the poem when Herrick borrows distinctly from Donne:

> . . . understand
> And know each wile,
> Each hieroglyphick of a kisse or smile;

This has behind it Donne's 'Elegie VII':

> . . . Foole, thou didst not understand
> The mystique language of the eye nor hand. . . .

But in doing this, Herrick was not aligning himself with the Metaphysicals. He was merely using the language Donne had made available for these occasions. And this was a habit most of the poets of the period acquired. It was as though Donne provided a stock of ready-tailored language and images from which a peculiarly mixed collection of writers borrowed whenever their own wit wore thin. 'Sons of Ben', like Cartwright and Suckling, plagiarized Donne without embarrassment and without in any way turning their poetical coats. I have even found a broadside poem, purporting to have been written by Thomas Wentworth, Earl of Strafford, just before his execution, in which are the lines:

> But O! how few there ar',
> (Though danger from that act be far)
> Will stoop and catch a falling star.[1]

Even at that critical moment, it appears, a quotation from Donne came pat. Judging, in fact, from the way phrases from Donne turn up again and again in unexpected places, it seems that his work was, as it were, a body of common knowledge to be drawn on whenever wit was needed, much as the eighteenth-century poets, when they wanted grandeur, turned to Milton.

[1] 'Verses, Lately written by Thomas Earle of *Strafford*', 1641. The broadside is in the Bodleian Library, Ashmole 1003.

II

Granted that Donne's poetry was there to be used for superficial effects by all comers, what was it that made a poet peculiarly a member of the School of Donne?

The nearer in time a writer was to Donne, the more metaphysical, in the straightforward and strict sense of that term, he was likely to be. For example, in 1601, when Donne's reputation as a young wit was fairly established (Everard Gilpin had 'borrowed' from him in print in 1598), a queer collection of poems called *Loves Martyr* appeared. The title poem was a long, dull piece by Robert Chester, but at the end of the volume was a collection of verse on the theme of the Phoenix and the Turtle by the most distinguished professional poets of the day: Shakespeare, Jonson, Chapman and Marston. It reads like the professionals' answer to Donne. None of the poems is 'conceited' in imagery, but they are all metaphysical in the other sense: analytic and peculiarly intellectual in tone and preoccupations. Shakespeare's 'The Phoenix and Turtle', in fact, seems to me more truly sustained and analytically metaphysical than anything Donne ever wrote.[2] None of these pieces belongs to the School of Donne in the literary historian's sense. But they show the kind of taste Donne's poetry had for the professionals of his time: dryer than I have been implying, but quite distinct.

Yet it is not the same distinctness that made Donne an important poet for his followers, still less for the twentieth century. I would call it a first impression Metaphysical style: the basic stuff of the verse is still largely traditional, but the surface has been altered. The poetry of Edward, Lord Herbert of Cherbury, the most senior member of the School of Donne, is also the most purely Metaphysical in this manner. And this may well be because he is also one of the least original personally. Donne's freshness and power, to put it naïvely, come from having so much that was original to say for himself; hence his impatience with the amatory pieties of his time. Herbert of Cherbury, on the other hand, has no quarrel at all with the emotional rhetoric of the Elizabethans. He merely tricks out their complacencies in a complicated logical pattern. He wrote no successful love poems, but he did write a number of relatively successful meditations on themes suggested by love.

[2] See my essay on the poem in *Interpretations*, ed. John Wain, 1955.

It is odd how Herbert of Cherbury manages to sound like Donne without having any of his realism. The personal pressure behind his poems seems, at best, mild, and the physical detail, metaphorical or otherwise, is sparse. What detail there is finds itself hurried, on the least provocation, into abstraction. Yet despite this, the poems are, in their rarefied way, extraordinarily accurate; and it is in this accuracy that they are influenced by Donne. Herbert may not question much personally, but he will let nothing be logically. Love, or the colour of his mistress's hair, or her physical coyness are all interesting for him not in themselves but as starting-points for accurate, elegant and complex arguments which end in an abstract but logically proved truth. Hence the whole burden of his poetry rests on the logical business. He does not 'feel his thoughts'; he abstracts his feelings. He is a perfect example not of the unified but of the dialectical sensibility.

It is important that Herbert's poems always seem to come to rest in some logically proved truth, for it is his preoccupation with truth, its conditions and its necessary logic, that gives Herbert that "metaphysical note . . . of tension or strain" which James Smith called the distinguishing mark of all this kind of poetry.[3] Herbert, as well as being a poet and a diplomat, was also something of a philosopher. He wrote a long, complicated and rather unoriginal disquistion on the subject of truth, *De Veritate*, the arguments and conclusions of which appear repeatedly in his more ambitious poems. Consider, for example, his one real masterpiece, with a very typical title: 'An Ode upon a Question moved, Whether Love should continue for ever?' It is a poem the Victorian scholars admired, and no one in this century has had a hard word for it. If you asked what, in fact, set it so much above the rest of Herbert's work, the answer would be, I suppose, that not only is the argument peculiarly delicate and subtle, even for Herbert, but, by using a dramatic setting, the poet has made the debate actual, characterized and to the point, instead of leaving it in the air as an abstract meditation; and he was prompted to this by Donne's 'The Extasie'.

Yet, when you really come to look at it, the scene-setting is not particularly striking, nor even particularly original. In fact, as physical description, it is rather vague:

> Having interr'd her Infant-birth,
>   The watry ground that late did mourn,
>   Was strew'd with flow'rs for the return
> Of the wish'd Bridegroom of the earth.

[3] 'On Metaphysical Poetry', *Determinations*, ed. F. R. Leavis, 1934.

The well accorded Birds did sing
  Their hymns unto the pleasant time,
  And in a sweet consorted chime
Did welcom in the chearful Spring.

To which, soft whistles of the Wind,
  And warbling murmurs of a Brook,
  And vari'd notes of leaves that shook,
An harmony of parts did bind.

While doubling joy unto each other,
  All in so rare concent was shown,
  No happiness that came alone,
Nor pleasure that was not another.

When with a love none can express,
  That mutually happy pair,
  Melander and *Celinda* fair,
The season with their loves did bless.

What comes over most strongly is not the descriptive detail
—'soft whistles of the Wind,/And warbling murmurs of a
Brook' are conventional enough—it is the *idea* of harmony.
This is repeated again and again: 'well accorded', 'sweet consorted', 'An harmony of parts', 'mutually happy'; and the
whole of the fourth stanza is devoted to the concept. Presumably, Herbert is emphasizing the perfection of Melander's
and Celinda's love. But he is also arranging the scene so
that it will support his conclusions about the truth of love.
For the whole thesis of *De Veritate* hinges on the question
of harmony. To give a very rough working generalization from
all windings of Herbert's arguments: truth is, first, a matter
of harmony between the beholder's inner faculties and the
exterior objects; second, there is a truth beyond this which
comes when the intellect has a harmonious understanding of
these minor truths of the faculties. Truth, in short, is a matter
of harmony between microcosm and macrocosm.

The relevance of all this to the poem is simply to show that
nothing, not even the setting, gets into the poem for its own
sake. Everything has a metaphysical justification. Consider,
for instance, that famous closing conceit:

This said, in her up-lifted face,
  Her eyes which did that beauty crown,
  Were like two starrs, that having faln down,
Look up again to find their place:

> While such a moveless silent peace
> Did seize on their becalmed sense,
> One would have thought some influence
> Their ravished spirits did possess.

It is, as Eliot said, 'lovely and justified'. But it also clinches the argument of the whole poem. *Melander* began his answer to the question moved with an invocation:

> O you, wherein, they say, Souls rest,
> Till they descend pure heavenly fires,
> Shall lustful and corrupt desires
> With your immortal seed be blest?

G. C. Moore Smith, the editor of the Oxford edition, has a note on this: "Souls, according to Plato's *Timaeus,* before their human birth were in the stars". Obliquely, then, by a reference to a philosopher, *Melander* has begun by invoking the stars as the original and pure home of the soul. And so when he has logically proved his point about the immortality of pure love, the stars inevitably return. Her eyes, the windows of the soul, are like 'faln stars' because her doubts have confined her to the limits of fallen humanity; his argument has restored their love to the eternal. Hence the triumphant moment of truth, of perfect harmony, the 'moveless silent peace'. The final image is justified and gains its place because of the argument; and the argument itself, like that image, depends on a kind of conceit from philosophy. To understand both, the reader is expected to have Plato at his fingertips.

This is both like and unlike Donne's practice: it is like in that to understand the poem fully the reader is expected to come fully prepared, knowing enough philosophy not to have to strain after the references. It is unlike in that all the details depend on the ideas behind them rather than on a personal and dramatic situation. Clearly, this has little to do with the kind of philosophizing that is to be found in Spenser: Herbert is not writing poetry which is, at one remove or another, *about* philosophy; he is writing, instead, *with* philosophy, using it for his own ends. But his ends are more immediately logical than personal. Herbert, in short, is Metaphysical in his manner of using a strict, insistent logic to impose an order on personal subjects, and in his way bolstering his logical proofs with unexplained and oblique references to other philosophy. But where Donne always gives the impression that the dialectic and metaphysics are utterly subservient to the present human situation, Herbert seems to use the situations as excuses for the rest of the philosophical business. Hence he is as content to borrow his subjects from the orthodox Elizabethans as from Donne.

III

Herbert's was a one-sided development of the style. Had it been the only development, Donne would have been a much less important force in English poetry than he is. But there were also writers who occasionally rose to what might be called the full Metaphysical style; that is, the style of King's 'Exequy', of Crashaw's verse-letter 'To the Countesse of Denbigh', and, with reservations, of Marvell's 'To his Coy Mistress'. All of these are masterpieces of the personal tone, yet none are idiosyncratic. In fact, the first two are hardly even characteristic of their authors: King was usually far milder and, like Herbert of Cherbury, far more at one with Elizabethan conventions; Crashaw was usually more excessive. Yet though these poems are their author's masterpieces they have fewest of their distinctive quirks. They are, someone once suggested, 'anonymous': less the product of a single man than of a style that was there to be used.

Yet they are also their author's masterpieces because quite simply, they are their most intelligent poems; not complex or intellectual, after the manner of Herbert of Cherbury, but intelligent in the fullest and most human sense. It is on this that Donne's enormous influence over English poetry depends. It has almost nothing to do with conceits, and not much to do with dialectic; but it has everything to do with a realism of the intelligence. Writing in this way left the poets little time to be strikingly idiosyncratic or coy or dull or over-intellectual. The best Metaphysical poetry is defined by the quality of full, tense but informal intelligence which it commands.

Compare, for example, two famous passages. This, from King's 'Exequy':

> Stay for me there; I will not faile
> To meet thee in that hollow Vale.
> And think not much of my delay;
> I am already on the way,
> And follow thee with all the speed
> Desire can make, or sorrows breed.
> Each minute is a short degree,
> And ev'ry houre a step towards thee.
> At night when I betake to rest,
> Next morn I rise neerer my West

Of life, almost by eight houres saile,
Then when sleep breath'd his drowsie gale.

Thus from the Sun my Bottom stears,
And my dayes Compass downward bears:
Nor labour I to stemme the tide
Through which to *Thee* I swiftly glide.

'Tis true, with shame and grief I yield,
Thou like the *Vann* first took'st the field,
And gotten hast the victory
In thus adventuring to dy
Before me, whose more years might crave
A just precedence in the grave.
But heark! My Pulse like a soft Drum
Beats my approach, tells *Thee* I come;
And slow howere my marches be,
I shall at last sit down by *Thee*.

And this from Donne's 'Elegie XVI':

O stay here, for, for thee
England is onely a worthie Gallerie,
To walke in expectation, till from thence
Our greatest King call thee to his presence.
When I am gone, dreame me some happinesse,
Nor let thy lookes our long hid love confesse,
Nor praise, nor dispraise me, nor blesse nor curse
Openly loves force, nor in bed fright thy Nurse
With midnights startings, crying out, oh, oh
Nurse, ô my love is slaine, I saw him goe
O'r the white Alpes alone; I saw him I,
Assail'd, fight, taken, stabb'd, bleed, fall, and die.
Augure me better chance, except dread *Iove*
Thinke it enough for me to'have had thy love.

In the abstract they are not very much alike. Donne's piece
is vivid, like so much of his work, because it is wholly and
clearly dramatized. This habit of presenting his feelings in
action, instead of sitting back and describing them, is the
key to Donne's immediacy. It also explains how he was able
to handle colloquial language with so little fuss: he seems
always to have been aware of the other people involved
in the scene; to be easy and natural was therefore a matter
of tact. King, on the other hand, does not work overtly
through a dramatic situation. Yet the two passages are alike

in tone: they have the same speed, concentration and actuality. This is partly a matter of language: both subdue the basic metre to the rhythm of speech, and at the same time they speak with an intensity that heightens the mere colloquialism until a genuine *rhythm* of speech appears. But it is partly a matter of the way King handles his metaphors: so directly and so immediately that they seem to be oblique and subdued dramatic situations which, therefore, demand the same intelligence and tact as is always at work in Donne's verse.

This is not, I think, a matter of genius for the extraordinary metaphor; if King had that he showed it nowhere else. It is rather a question of a certain vitality of interest over an unusually large range of, in these poetical matters, unexpected subjects. The poet feels wholly at his ease in referring to any realm that the intelligent, educated man would know for himself: navigation, law, commerce, science, warfare, philosophy. He presumes less on learning, in the rather specialized manner of Herbert of Cherbury, Cleveland or, at the other end of the scale, Spenser, than on a depth and sophistication of interest. The dramatic power and ease of his writing is directly proportional to the sane vitality of his interest. It is this that adds up to that impression of realistic intelligence. He writes not as a poet committed only to the world of literature and myth but as, in the best sense, a man of the world, who responds as immediately to politics, business and the sciences as to the arts. At its best, Metaphysical poetry comes very close to the tone of Shakespeare's Roman plays. It is for this reason that I tried to show that Donne's style was based on the interests of the most intelligent professional men of his time, instead of on the more technical interests of the professional poets. The purest Metaphysical style is the intimate voice and formulation of the most intelligent professional class at the moment in English literature when even the professional class was creative.

IV

I suggested that there were three main classes of poets who adapted Donne's style to their own ends: the courtiers, the divines and the University Wits. Yet, in fact, the 'metaphysical note' is sounded in much the same way by all of them. There is almost a formula for it:

Aske me no more where Jove bestowes,
When June is past, the fading rose . . .

I cannot tell who loves the Skeleton
Of a poor Marmoset, nought but boan, boan . . .

Tell me no more how fair she is . . .

What if he had been tabled at thy teats? . . .

Aske the empress of the night
How the Hand which guides her sphere,
Constant in unconstant light,
Taught the waves her yoke to bear . . .

Tell me, O tell, what kind of thing is *Wit* . . .

Those lines are by an average cross-section of the School:
by Carew, Lovelace, King, Crashaw, Thomas Stanley and
Cowley respectively. The formula is to begin with a question, usually personal, complex and concerning the emotions,
and then to answer it with a considerable show of logic,
bolstering the argument with occasional conceits; so, as an
answer, the poem ends in a dialectical and emotional point
of rest. The formula, of course, was first Donne's:

I wonder by my troth, what thou, and I
Did, till we lov'd? . . .

All true Metaphysical poems might be subtitled 'An Ode
upon a Question moved'.

With the courtly poets, however, the final effect of the
procedure is to produce poems rather different from those of
the other Metaphysicals. Consider, for example, the odd lists
of scientific knowledge which turn up continually in Caroline
court poetry, even at its smoothest and most stylish:

Aske me no more where *Jove* bestowes,
When *June* is past, the fading rose:
For in your beauties orient deepe,
These flowers as in their causes, sleepe.

Those 'causes', say the notes, come from Aristotle's *Physics*,
and their use is precise and appropriate. The gesture is very
much in the manner of Donne, but the effect is different.
For it has none of the personal charge Donne put on his

learning, nothing that had to do with 'an Hydroptique immoderate desire of humane learning and languages'. Instead, the learning has become part of a more diffuse air of knowingness. Carew uses it to strengthen his questioning sophistication.

The same elegant knowingness dominates when the courtly poets followed Donne in the dramatic openings of their poems. Again I will use Carew, since he is the most original of the Carolines, but nearly all of them, from Feltham to Fanshaw, were essentially the same when they imitated Donne:

> Thinke not cause men flatt'ring say,
> Y're fresh as Aprill, sweet as May,
> Bright as is the morning starre,
> That thou art so . . .

> Know *Celia,* (since thou art so proud,)
> 'Twas I that gave thee thy renowne . . .

> Now you have freely given me leave to love
> What will you doe? . . .

As *vers donnés* they yield very little to Donne in the way of freshness and originality. But with Donne the initial discovery at its best suggests a new truth about the feelings which the rest of the poem then substantiates, whereas Carew and the others use their brilliant openings simply as a means of striking an attitude. From that position of security they debate, but they move forward very little. Their stylishness, in fact, has an almost static formality. It can be seen in their language which, even when colloquial, is always highly polished; they rarely risk Donne's metrical irregularities. It can be seen, too, in a certain elegance in their references; their learning is always fitted so perfectly to the case in hand that, though it adds point to their scepticism, it rarely generates any power of its own. Finally and above all, it can be seen in that slight detachment which makes their love poems, for all their subtle intimacies, seem part of a sophisticated but set amatory procedure. "The formality of their language", Marius Bewley once wrote, "and the definition which the Court provided for their attitudes enabled them, with this intricate instrument, to keep a certain distance between themselves and their feelings, a distance which allowed various shades of cynicism or detachment to circulate freely around their verbal statements." [4]

Mr Bewley was prompted to this excellent formulation partly by an analysis of Lovelace's masterpiece, 'La Bella Bona-Roba':

> I cannot tell who loves the Skeleton
> Of a poor Marmoset, nought but boan, boan.
> Give me a nakednesse with her cloath's on.
>
> Such whose white-sattin upper coat of skin,
> Cut upon Velvet rich Incarnadin,
> Ha's yet a Body (and of Flesh) within.
>
> Sure it is meant good Husbandry in men,
> Who do incorporate with Aery leane,
> T'repair their sides, and get their Ribb agen.
>
> Hard hap unto that Huntsman that Decrees
> Fat joys for all his swet, when as he sees
> After this 'say, nought but his Keepers fees.
>
> Then Love I beg, when next thou tak'st thy Bow,
> Thy angry shafts, and dost Heart-chasing go,
> Passe Rascall Deare, strike me the largest Doe.

It is a brilliant but oddly unsatisfactory poem; unsatisfactory because, despite Mr Bewley's sensitive analysis, and despite the poet's show of logic (the 'sures' and 'thens'), the poem seems very little sustained or even argued out. On the contrary, it is curiously static. The impetus behind it, which imparts that extraordinarily disturbed rhythm to the opening stanza, is not a mere preference for fat women; it is instead the shock of being reminded of death, of seeing the skeleton, at the moment of sexual attraction. The real poem, in fact, is over by the end of the first stanza, when Lovelace counteracts this shock by adopting an almost aggressive attitude of defence:

> Give me a nakednesse with her cloath's on.

After this he merely substantiates this attitude by three clever and elaborate conceits—though the third at least is conventional enough. He embroiders but does not change what he

[4] 'The Colloquial Mode of Byron', *Scrutiny*, XVI, 1949, p. 22.

has already stated so categorically. He uses his wit, in fact, to preserve his balance, not to help him towards some new resolution.

If 'La Bella Bona-Roba', like most courtly Metaphysical verse, seems static in comparison with Donne's work, that is not because the writer lacks a vitality of wit. It is rather that his poetic energy has gone elsewhere. The courtiers' criterion is not wit used to bring into control recalcitrant personal material, but wit as a quality to be exercised and enjoyed for itself. The whole of Lovelace's poem, for example, could be justified as an elaborate extension of a pun: both 'Bona-Roba' and 'marmoset' were seventeenth-century euphemisms for 'prostitute'. Instead of the drive of Donne's full, difficult, logical honesty, the courtiers seemed to value above all the accomplishment with which their knowledge and ingenuity were used so easily and precisely, the delicacy with which they balanced their arguments and examples. What makes the poems move is the poets' enjoyment in their own performance. This is not to imply that they never took their wit seriously. They could hardly have written so well if they hadn't. But their seriousness and effort went into preserving a courtly stance of formal, polished detachment. It is these poets who, even while seeming to write like Donne, foreshadowed the elegant and more social wit of the Augustans.

Chapter Three

THE POETRY OF RELIGIOUS EXPERIENCE

I.   GEORGE HERBERT

DONNE'S influence has been so firmly associated with a certain intellectual bravura that the wider effects of his realism have scarcely been noticed. The only poet to use Donne's discoveries for wholly original ends was George Herbert; and his ends were so far from the conventional witty detachment that his reputation has suffered.

He has never really escaped the nineteenth-century rôle of the simple, quaint and 'pious rector of Bemerton', for whom even Grierson could only say: "if not greatly imaginative, Herbert is a sincere and sensitive poet, and an accomplished artist elaborating his argumentative strain or little allegories and conceits with felicitous completeness, and managing his variously patterned stanzas . . . with a finished and delicate harmony. *The Temple* breathes the spirit of the Anglican Church at its best, primitive and modest; and also of one troubled and delicate soul seeking and finding peace." [1] This is the best that could be said for him. It is not much. Even when the Metaphysicals once more became the fashion, Herbert received relatively little of the attention. Granted L. C. Knights and William Empson have written better on Herbert than on any other poet; but there is little else of importance. If Herbert has had any status in the revival of the School of Donne, that is more because he was Metaphysical than because he was an original artist in his own right. Now that the Metaphysicals are once more falling out of fashion there is a new movement to get Herbert's poetry back wholly into the Church; the latest studies of his poetry have emphasized their pattern of meditation, their ecclesiastical symbolism and emblems, their relation to the liturgy—in short, their piety, in a new and more technical form than before. In this, he is now said to have been influenced as much by Robert Southwell and Sir Philip Sidney as by Donne. Herbert has never really been acquitted

[1] *Metaphysical Lyrics and Poems of the Seventeenth Century,* ed. H. J. C. Grierson, Oxford, 1921, p. xliv.

of Grierson's regretful charge: "the effect is a little stuffy".

He has, in fact, been consistently unlucky, even in his own time. Although he was twenty years younger than Donne, he died within two years of him and their poems were both first published posthumously in the same year. Inevitably, Herbert's were overshadowed. His poetic reputation, even then, depended more on his piety than his originality.

He owes, of course, a good deal to Donne, but his debt is nowhere as specific as that of the other Metaphysicals. Like all of them, he borrows from time to time, but that is not important. What matters more is that he rises occasionally to Donne's peculiar intensity, which is a question less of phraseology than of movement. When, for example, Herbert writes:

> I have consider'd it, and finde
> There is no dealing with thy mighty passion:
> For though I die for thee, I am behinde;
> My sinnes deserve the condemnation.
>
> ('The Reprisall')

What he is saying is his own, but that particularly powerful manner of saying would not have been possible without the example of Donne's *Holy Sonnets*:

> Oh, to vex me, contraryes meet in one . . .

Before Donne there had been in English powerful liturgical poetry; the greatest theological poetry, Milton's, was still to come; but devotional poetry that was not concerned with the 'public' occasions of religion had never risen above relatively formal rhetorical conventions. Donne was the first to write with a rhythmic tightness and force which could express the peculiarly tense, energetic and slightly intellectual despair of religious conflict. The same realism which made his love poems different from any that had gone before created, when used for other ends, a new mode: a poetry of religious experience.

It was Herbert, however, who from this initial impulse of Donne's produced a common language for religious verse. The line runs directly from him rather than from Donne. Vaughan owes Herbert an enormous debt; so, though less obviously, does Traherne; Crashaw called his volume *Steps to the Temple,* in deference to Herbert's *The Temple;* other minor seventeenth-century poets invoked him or his book in the same way. And the great religious poet of the nineteenth century, Hopkins, acknowledged Herbert as one of his masters. The difference in surfaces—Hopkins's elaborate complexity and Herbert's equally elaborate simplicity—is endless; but they are both alike in their underlying determination to plot the stresses of religious conflicts as they are rather than as they should be. And occasionally, when Hopkins's overbearing isolation was his theme rather than a force acting obliquely on his poetic technique, they sound alike:

> Thou art indeed just, Lord, if I contend
> With thee; but, sir, so what I plead is just.

The tone and movement are very close to "I have consider'd it, and finde". . . .

Herbert's influence, however, is something more plottable than 'tone and movement'. The critics agree that his strength lies in what Coleridge called his "pure, manly, and unaffected diction". His editor, Dr Hutchinson, added that he learned this easy, conversational language from Donne. But Herbert does not write simply because he restricts himself to simple subjects and simple statements about them; because, as the legend goes, the essence of his poetry is an unquestioning piety which is occasionally put off centre by his taste for the quaint. On the contrary, his simplicity is the outcome of a great deal of concentration. Instead of cutting down the stuff of his poetry to suit his style, Herbert writes with a clarity that includes the discordant elements and transcends them. His simplicity is not the measure by which he fell short of Donne, but of the distance he went beyond him. It is also the measure of Herbert's influence on the devotional poets who followed him. For Donne's realism was controlled by a sensibility that was so instinctively dialectical and learned that it was too easily taken to be something rather specialized. Metaphysical poetry, in fact, declined because Donne's style was used merely as a formula for self-conscious wit-writing. Herbert, on the other hand, disciplined abilities almost as great as Donne's to less striking ends. The result was he created an idiom which could be used by poets who, in terms of dialectic and learning, may have been less gifted but were not a jot less concerned with the sharpness and force of their religious conflicts.

There are four ways of showing that Herbert's simplicity was a quality complex in itself and attained with great difficulty. First, he wrote about it more or less explicitly; second, he controlled it by deflecting his wit into skills which would enhance rather than ruffle the clear surface of his work; third, he set his specialized learning against a larger background of belief; finally, he based this simplicity on a whole style of behaviour; on manners, that is, rather than on a literary manner.

In his important essay,[2] Professor Knights called Herbert's two 'Jordan' poems his "literary manifesto". They are his farewell to poetical fashions: to allegory, pastoral, verbal obliquity and complication. But with a difference; his method itself is oblique:

> Who sayes that fictions onely and false hair
> Become a verse? Is there in truth no beautie?
> Is all good structure in a winding stair?
> May no lines passe, except they do their dutie
>   Not to a true, but painted chair? . . .
>
> Shepherds are honest people; let them sing:
> Riddle who list, for me, and pull for Prime:
> I envie no mans nightingale or spring;
> Nor let them punish me with losse of rime,
>   Who plainly say, *My God, My King*.

The poem has puzzled the critics, more or less mildly, ever since Herbert's first detailed commentator, George Ryley, wrote about it in 1714, in his long, dull, unpublished, but determinedly analytical book: *Mr Herbert's Temple/ & Church Militant/ Explained & Improved/ By/ A Discourse upon Each Poem/ Critical/ & / Practical*:

> There is some Difficulty in Reconciling the Titles with ye subject matt^e of ye Poems. Each Poem is an Invective ag^st Dark Poetry; w^ch, by figures, etc, rend^e ye Sence of ye Poem, & ye Drift of ye Author obscure; & to Common Ears Unintelligible. I am ready to say the Author has, in these, Lash'd himself; by prefixing a title y^t either is, or att Least, is to me very obscure. . . . Here are 9 or 10 exp^esions y^t may want opening enough to make so short a poem fall und^e ye charge, it draw up ag^st others . . .[3]

[2] In *Explorations*, 1946.

[3] Bodleian MS. Rawl. D. 199, p. 69. The manuscript is dated March ye 24, 171 4/5. I have been unable to find out anything about George Ryley, but surmise, from his thorough and up-to-date knowledge of theology and from his didactic intentions and air, that he was a cleric of some kind.

The charge is, simply, that Herbert's defence of plainness is also one of the most obscure poems he wrote. There is, of course, an excuse: perhaps Herbert was attacking the vice by parodying it. Yet the elaborations are built up so easily, so convincingly, that Herbert seems less to be criticizing witty elaboration than using the occasion to indulge in it. He has, in short, a natural sophistication and a natural penchant for complexity which he was at pains to discipline into simplicity. I repeat *into,* for he did not get rid of these qualities; he used them in another way.

How and why he did so are the subject of 'The Fore-runners', a poem, in its way, almost as finely dramatic as anything of Donne's:

> The harbingers are come. See, see their mark;
> White is their colour, and behold my head.
> But must they have my brain? must they dispark
> Those sparkling notions, which therein were bred?
>   Must dulnesse turn me to a clod?
> Yet they have left me, *Thou art still my God.*
>
> Good men ye be, to leave me my best room,
> E'en all my heart, and what is lodged there:
> I pass not, I, what of the rest become,
> So, *Thou art still my God,* be out of fear.
>   He will be pleased with that ditty;
> And if I please him, I write fine and witty.
>
> Farewell sweet phrases, lovely metaphors.
> But will ye leave me thus? when ye before
> Of stews and brothels onely knew the doores,
> Then did I wish you with my tears, and more,
>   Brought you to Church well drest and clad:
> My God must have my best, ev'n all I had.
>
> Lovely enchanting language, sugarcane,
> Honey of roses, whither wilt thou fly?
> Hath some fond lover 'ticed thee to thy bane?
> And wilt thou leave the Church, and love a sty?
>   Fy, thou wilt soil thy broider'd coat,
> And hurt thyself, and him that sings the note. . . .
>
> Yet, if you go, I passe not; take your way:
> For, *Thou art still my God,* is all that ye
> Perhaps with more embellishment can say.
> Go birds of spring: let winter have his fee;

> Let a bleake palenesse chalke the doore,
> So all within be livelier than before.

The difference between this and the 'Jordan' poems is a matter of its point in time. In 'Jordan' Herbert wrote of the simple style as though it were a willed deprivation, a kind of penance for inventiveness. The choice was either religion *or* wit, devotion *or* invention; either he said "My God, My King" *or* he riddled in sweet phrases. This clash of styles echoed the clash between his secular ambition and his piety. If there is at times something rather self-conscious or over-deliberate in Herbert's earlier simplicity, that is perhaps because the habits of his career died hard.

He was, of course, far from being a simple country parson, however saintlike his later years may have been. He came from a talented and distinguished family. He became Public Orator of Cambridge when he was twenty-six and because of 'his great abilities' was, his biographer Walton says, "very high in the King's favour, and not meanly valued and loved by the most eminent and most powerful of the Court Nobility".[4] Donne, Henry Wotton, Lancelot Andrewes and Bacon were his friends. He helped translate *The Advancement of Learning* into a 'masculine' style of Latin; in return Bacon dedicated to him his *Translation of Certaine Psalmes into English Verse* (1625).

Naturally enough with these talents he appears, from what his biographers say, to have been extremely ambitious, as Donne had been. And like Donne, he took Holy Orders only after a period of intense personal suffering which came on him when the massive progress of his secular career faltered. It was perhaps the clash between his ambition and his piety that created the analytical tension out of which most of his best poems were written. Herbert himself suggested as much when, as he was dying, he sent the manuscript book of his poems to Nicholas Ferrar, saying that "he shall find there in it a picture of the many spiritual Conflicts that have past betwixt God and my Soul, before I could subject mine to the will of Jesus my Master, in whose service I have now found perfect freedom".[5] But the repose of a fulfilled and reconciled simplicity seems to have come relatively late. He had not, I think, achieved it when he wrote the two 'Jordan'

---

[4] *Walton's Lives*, with an Introduction and Notes by S. B. Carter, 1951, p. 213.

[5] Walton, *loc. cit.*, p. 252.

poems.[6] On the contrary, their disproportionately stylish complexity makes sense only as Herbert's way of showing that he was as much a master of the riddling, embellished manner he had renounced as any elegant and successful courtier. But by the time he wrote 'The Forerunners' he had made his peace with form and content:

> Let a bleak palenesse chalk the doore,
> So all within be livelier than before.

The new simplicity of his style was the outer form of a new richness of life. It is very much to the point that 'The Forerunners' is both about writing poetry and growing old. His simplicity is a spiritual quality, the measure of his maturity as a poet.

There is a difference, however, between simplicity and deprivation. Herbert's work may be lucid, controlled, precise, but it is far from being stripped down to its bare essentials. The wit remains, though in a rather transmuted form. His poetry has none of Donne's occasionally ostentatious dialectical brilliance nor of the courtier-poet's elegant supersophistication. Herbert's wit and ingenuity went, instead, into his verse-forms. He invented an enormous number of them and rarely bothered to repeat a discovery. Perhaps he was helped to this fecundity by his well-known skill in music. But there is a kind of ingenious stylishness in his metres that seems to me to depend as much on sharpness of mind as of ear:

> Come dearest Lord, passe not this holy season,
> My flesh and bones and joynts do pray:
> And e'vn my verse, when by the ryme and reason
> The word is, *Stay,* sayes ever, *Come.*

That is from a poem called 'Home'. So by transposing the rhyme word Herbert not merely puts a sudden stress on his plea, he also makes the plea itself bring back the subject of the poem: 'Come' rhymes with 'Home'. The metrical forms, in short, bear the weight of a good deal of the wit which would not otherwise have been proper to his subject.

---

[6] 'The Forerunners' appears in the large Bodleian MS. but not in the Williams MS. So it is presumably later than the 'Jordan' poems, which are in both. See F. E. Hutchinson's introduction to *The Works of George Herbert*, Oxford, 1953, pp. l-lvi; also his article on 'George Herbert' in *Seventeenth Century Studies Presented to Sir Herbert Grierson*, Oxford, 1938, pp. 149-53, 158.

As with his wit, so with his learning. Herbert's career and his reputation among his contemporaries show that in plain ability he was probably not so very much behind Donne, although the uses he put his talents to were rather less spectacular. In that beautiful poem 'The Pearl', he drew up his personal credit, fully and without false modesty, in order to dignify his love of God by his renunciation of mere worldly abilities. The list begins:

> I know the wayes of Learning; both the head
> And pipes that feed the presse, and make it runne;
> What reason hath from nature borrowed,
> Or of it self, like a good huswife, spunne
> In laws and policie; what the starres conspire,
> What willing nature speaks, what forc'd by fire;
> Both th'old discoveries, and the new-found seas,
> The stock and surplus, cause and historie:
> All these stand open, or I have the keyes:
>
> > Yet I love thee.

The list is presumably as inclusive as Donne's would have been; yet though Herbert deploys his learning skilfully throughout his work, it nowhere assumes the central importance of Donne's. For example, in *Les doctrines médiévales chez Donne* Miss M. P. Ramsay decided that Donne was a mediaeval thinker; her evidence was his modes of thinking and his use of the scholastic philosophers. One could prove nothing of the kind of Herbert, despite a command of argument no less accurate and something of the same ease in making his way among the authorities. For to call a Jacobean poet 'mediaeval' is to impute to him a kind of specialization—which was precisely what happened to Donne. But Herbert's poetry is not specialized in this way, although he may have been a product of no less specialized a training. The reason is that the general and dominant framework of his work is not his University learning but, quite simply, the Bible. And the Bible, like the Church liturgy which he also used, was easily and readily available to any devout reader. Even Mr George Ryley managed to make adequate, if uninspired sense of the poems merely by pointing out the Biblical references.

This framework helped Herbert to his simplicity in a number of ways. First, it took away all strain from the references; to understand Herbert was not necessarily a token of the reader's wit. Second, it gave his conceits, although they may owe something to the emblem writers, a homelier directness than Donne's; their force is like that of the parables or, as Professor Knights suggested, of popular pulpit oratory. (It may be that this kind of directness was something of a mixed blessing for Herbert. His failures are nearly all of the homely and hortatory kind. When the cast of a poem is purely that of the teacher, benign and clear-cut, a certain didactic monotony intrudes. The work becomes tiresome whenever the poet seems insistently to be writing at less than full pitch.) The third benefit Herbert's poetry gained from the Bible was its air of finality. At his best—in, say, the first 'Affliction'— Herbert's self-examination and psychological analysis was no less than Donne's, but it was presented within the context of an answer. Donne was continually arguing out his position with God in such a way as to make one believe that there was a good deal to be said on both sides. Herbert, on the other hand, presented his emotional conflicts from the vantage point of their outcome; that is, with a certain finality. It is this that makes the turn-abouts at the end of 'Affliction I' and 'The Pulley' inevitable, given the poet's kind of mature and critical humility. But to this, of course, the Bible is only ancillary; the controlling power is Herbert's depth of understanding of his own experience.

These, then, are the technical or semi-technical inducements to simplicity; but its essence lies elsewhere: in Herbert's power of implication. In this his learning and intellectual complexities were less important than what Professor Knights, in a peculiarly suggestive paragraph, called 'the well-bred ease of manner of "the gentleman" '. Herbert mentioned it himself in 'The Pearl':

> I know the wayes of Honour, what maintains
>   The quick returns of courtesie and wit . . .

The fullness of Herbert's poetry depends finally, I think, on his constant assumption of manners as a way of expressing not forms and formalities but an implicit fullness of life, a quickness of response and sensitivity. He can leave so much unsaid because his tone implies it all for him:

> Love bade me welcome: yet my soul drew back,
>   Guiltie of dust and sinne.
> But quick-ey'd Love, observing me grow slack
>   From my first entrance in,
> Drew nearer to me, sweetly questioning,
>   If I lack'd any thing.
> A guest, I answer'd, worthy to be here:

> Love said, You shall be he:
> I the unkinde, ungratefull? Ah my deare,
> I cannot look on thee.
> Love took my hand, and smiling did reply,
> Who made the eyes but I?
>
> Truth Lord, but I have marr'd them: let my shame
> Go where it doth deserve.
> And know you not, sayes Love, who bore the blame?
> My deare, then I will serve.
> You must sit down, sayes Love, and taste my meat:
> So I did sit and eat.

This is the last poem in *The Temple* and it treats the book's most important subject: the final acceptance of the love of God. But it does so in terms of, in the best sense, manners. The relationship of the poet to his God is that of a guest to his host. On this metaphor the whole poem is based. Love, given social graces and made to use polite formulae: "Love bade me welcome . . ."; "quick-ey'd Love . . . Drew nearer to me, sweetly questioning,/If I lack'd any thing"; "Love took my hand, and smiling did reply . . . (with, incidentally, an elegant-serious pun); "You must sit down, sayes Love, and taste my meat". The poet, too, reacts as a guest, according to the code: he is not clean enough to sit at table, being "Guiltie of *dust* and sinne"; he refuses because he senses a certain rude inadequacy in himself, but accepts directly his refusal itself begins to seem impolite. The balance is delicate and I describe it badly. The essence of the poem is a kind of understood tenderness. The social metaphor in no way makes the poem stiff, unreal or debilitatingly formal; it is, instead, a means of implying a great deal without ever overstating. Certainly, it does not stop the poet speaking out:

> "I the unkinde, ungratefull? Ah my deare,
> I cannot look on thee."

The intensity of this depends on the control that both precedes and follows it. It has, I think, the same force as that scene at the end of James's *The Awkward Age* when Nanda, after a whole volume of understatement, breaks down for a moment and weeps, so that one realizes suddenly the depth of feeling the polite formulas have, all the time, been covering. Herbert's simplicity, then, is deep and complex because it is born not of bareness but of tact. He knows how to judge to the last degree the feeling implicit in simple, even conventional, phrases.

The difference between this and earlier religious poetry is obvious when one compares Herbert's 'Love (III)' with the passage from Robert Southwell's *S. Peters Complaint* on which it may be based:

> At sorrowes dore I knockt, they crau'd my name;
> I aunswered one, vnworthy to be knowne:
> What one, say they? one worthiest of blame.
> But who? a wretch, not Gods, nor yet his owne.
> A man? O no, a beast; much worse: what creature?
> A rocke: how cald? the rocke of scandale, Peter.[7]

Compared with the beautifully balanced give and take of Herbert's poem Southwell's is crude and his self-degradation rhetorical. The more it grows, the more inhuman and unreal it becomes:

> A man? O no, a beast; much worse: what creature?
> A rocke. . . .

With the instrument of rhetoric, the stronger the religious emotion, the farther it retires from the world of common feelings into the world of allegory, formal and apart. Herbert, on the other hand, even at his worst retires no farther than parable, the simple, more or less vivid tale with an immediate application to the life around him.

I suggested that the power Donne exerted was towards realism and away from the formally poetical. But Donne's realism was of the professional classes, the lawyers, diplomats and the rest, who were intellectual, learned, active and sharp. Herbert translated this to fit his milder, more reposedly devotional sensibility and the easier, more courtly-polite background in which he lived out much of his life. The result was a realism on slightly different terms: a realism based on manners rather than dialectic.

But just as Donne's realism transcended mere logic and intellectualism, so Herbert's went beyond its allegiances to a code of manners, to the Bible, to parables and pulpit oratory. Both of them wrote, in an age of theology, a poetry of direct religious experience:

[7] Quoted by F. E. Hutchinson, *The Works of George Herbert*, Oxford, 1953, p. 543.

> And now in age I bud again,
> After so many deaths I live and write;
> I once more smell the dew and rain,
> And relish versing: O my onely light,
>> It cannot be
>> That I am he
> On whom thy tempests fell all night.

This is, I suppose, the most perfect and most vivid stanza in the whole of Herbert's work. But it is, in every sense, so natural that its originality is easily missed. To speak of the love of God as a *whole* delight, of the senses as much as of the spirit, had to my knowledge never been done before. To do it there was needed a combination of realism and personal tact that was Herbert's special gift.[8] His contribution to religious poetry is large and his own. But the ground in which it could flower had been cleared by Donne.

II. HENRY VAUGHAN

Eliot, defending Herbert against the claims of Vaughan, once concluded: "In short, the emotion of Herbert is clear, definite, mature and sustained; whereas the emotion of Vaughan is vague, adolescent, fitful and retrogressive".[9] Admittedly, he straightaway added: "This judgment is excessively harsh"; nevertheless, Eliot's was a fair reaction to the Vaughan irritant. And this is not wholly Vaughan's fault: he has been used by Wordsworth enthusiasts who imagined they saw in him intimations of the nature-childhood cult; he has been used as an example of the poetic powers of religion, whence the endless haggling over the date of his conversion and the usually sterile discussion of his mysticism; and he has been used by historians of ideas

---

[8] This devotion strengthened by the senses was not the only form his realism took. There is a strange poem called 'Perseverance', which appears in the Williams MS. but not in the printed version of *The Temple*, and which seems to be doing something rather different again:
> Onely my soule hangs on thy promises
> With face and hands clinging vnto thy brest,
> Clinging and crying, crying without cease,
> Thou art my rock, thou art my rest.

This seems to me an extraordinary attempt to catch what might be called the rhythm of prayer without following the usual patterns of meditation. Hutchinson does not explain why Herbert discarded the lines from his final collection. Perhaps it was because the poem was an experiment.

[9] T. S. Eliot, 'The Silurist', *The Dial*, LXXXIII, 1927, p. 263.

more interested in his Hermetical doctrines than in the poetry in which they were embodied. But the irritant is also in Vaughan himself. There seems no reason for him to be as good a poet as he sometimes is. His early poems are very much those of a minor talent. They were pleasant, dapper and derivative. He modelled himself, without much conviction, on the writers then in fashion, occasionally, like everyone else, stealing from Donne, but more consistently from Habington, with snatches of Randolph, Feltham and Waller.[10] His work was polished and quite clever, but also quite as empty as that particular brand of elegance required. Even *Silex Scintillans,* the volume on which Vaughan's reputation depends, is derivative in a quite unprecedented way. "He follows", said Dr Hutchinson, "only too closely Herbert's subjects and titles, and incorporates into his verse a number, past reckoning, of quotations, conscious and unconscious, from the *Temple* poems. . . . There is no example in English literature of one poet adopting another poet's works so extensively." [11]

I will not be dealing with Vaughan's use of Hermetical philosophy, nor with his mysticism, nor with his plagiarisms, nor even with his imagery. All these have been authoritatively written up by Frank Kermode.[12] I am interested in what, in its patchy way, underlies all these: his originality. And this worked best in precisely the same realm as Herbert's, that of the poetry of religious experience—or, since I can't pretend to criticize specifically religious excellence and originality, a poetry of experience with devotional themes.

Although Vaughan credited both his religious and his poetic conversion to Herbert's influence, [13] and although there is hardly a poem by him that doesn't contain an echo of Herbert, his sensibility was quite unlike that of any of the other Metaphysicals', Herbert's included. He was in no way a wit; if he had been, his early 'witty' poems could never have been so dull. In some ways he had more in common with the learned clergymen who used to edit him than with any of the school of Donne. He lived in comparative isolation; he called himself *Henry Vaughan, Silurist;* he translated out-of-the-way Latin authors and wrote a *Life of Blessed Paulinus,*

10 See F. E. Hutchinson, *Henry Vaughan,* Oxford 1947, pp. 50-1.

11 *The Works of George Herbert,* ed. F. E. Hutchinson, Oxford, 1941, pp. xli-xlii.

12 'The Private Imagery of Henry Vaughan', *Review of English Studies,* N.S., I, 1950, pp. 206-25.

13 See 'The Author's Preface' to *Silex Scintillans* in *Vaughan's Works,* ed. L. C. Martin, Oxford, 1914, II, p. 391.

Bishop of Nola; he dabbled in Hermetical Physic, practised medicine and was litigious. With less intelligence, and writing in a style that insisted less on intelligence, he might have been a crank living in an interesting but impenetrable private world. But he wasn't: his poems are public and intelligent. The difference between Vaughan and his predecessors—Herbert and *a fortiori* Donne—was one of innocence.

Both Herbert and Vaughan, for example, often use the things and creatures of Nature as starting-points for religious poems. They describe, say, a flower, and then apply the description. It is a perfectly orthodox formula. But Herbert uses Nature always with an element of what I called 'manners'. Even the

> Sweet rose, whose hue angrie and brave
> Bids the rash gazer wipe his eye;

for all the tenderness of the description, has a second root somewhere in the polite, social world It behaves. In comparison, Vaughan seems at first far more a poet of the intuitions writing, at his best, with a strong feeling for the thing as it is in itself. I do not in fact think this is true, or, in that age, could have been true; the formal requirements of poetry were too great. But something peculiarly original does happen when Vaughan writes of Nature. A couple of examples are needed at this point. First, the start of 'The Timber':

> Sure thou didst flourish once! and many Springs,
> Many bright mornings, much dew, many showers
> Past ore thy head: many light *Hearts* and *Wings*
> Which now are dead, lodg'd in thy living bowers.
>
> And still a new succession sings and flies;
> Fresh Groves grow up, and their green branches shoot
> Towards the old and still enduring skies,
> While the low *Violet* thrives at their root.
>
> But thou beneath the sad and heavy *Line*
> Of death, dost waste all senseless, cold and dark;
> Where not so much as dreams of light may shine,
> Nor any thought of greenness, leaf or bark.
>
> And yet (as if some deep hate and dissent,
> Bred in thy growth betwixt high winds and thee,
> Were still alive) thou dost great storms resent
> Before they come, and know'st how near they be.

> Else all at rest thou lyest, and the fierce breath
> Of tempests can no more disturb thy ease;
> But this thy strange resentment after death
> Means onely those, who broke (in life) thy peace.
>
> So murthered man, when lovely life is done,
> And his blood freez'd, keeps in the Center still
> Some secret sense, which makes the dead blood run
> At his approach, that did the body kill. . . .

Without a title, it would be hard to see what the piece is about. Yet the pattern itself is conventional: an example expounded and applied (the next stanza begins:

> And is there any murth'rer worse then sin?
> Or any storms more foul than a lewd life?).

It is the writing that is by no means conventional; instead it is almost disproportionately powerful and detailed. This is not because Vaughan has somehow entered into the nature of the timbering which creaks at the approach of bad weather. It is, instead, because he is expressing, with extraordinary inwardness, his own sense of sin. Not that the timber is a *persona* for his own sharp feelings; rather, he *creates his feelings* in terms of his subject. Hence not only is there a certain formality given to his own inner perceptions, but he is able to use them for the more obvious didactic ends that were expected of this kind of poetry.

These sharp, odd feelings often became entangled with Vaughan's theories. The extraordinary opening of 'Cockcrowing', for example:

> Father of lights! what Sunnie seed,
> What glance of day hast thou confin'd
> Into this bird? To all the breed
> This busie Ray thou hast assign'd;
>   Their magnetisme works all night,
>   And dreams of Paradise and light.

Mr Kermode has shown how 'magnetisme' fits in with Vaughan's Hermetic dabbling. But it is equally important to remember that the word is used with particularly little technical fuss. The stanza does not centre on 'magnetisme'. Instead, it depends, in the best lyric manner, on the opening exclamation: 'Father of lights!' The poet then goes on to define and clarify his feelings about God as light. The 'glance of day' and 'dreams of Paradise and light' do just as much as the idea of magnetism to define the kind of feeling he has for his subject.

This question of the immediate feelings is central to Vaughan's originality. Despite all his borrowings, his work is full of lines which could have been written by no one else:

> "I see them walking in an Air of glory,
> Whose light doth *trample* on my days:"

> "Just so it is in death. But thou
> Shalt in thy mothers bosome sleepe
> Whilst I each minute *grone* to know
> How neere Redemption *creepes.*"

> "But felt through all this fleshly dresse
> Bright *shootes* of everlastingnesse."

> "O then how bright
> And quick a light
> Doth *brush* my heart and scatter night;"

> "I cannot reach it; and my *striving* eye
> *Dazles* at it, as at eternity." [My italics]

Vaughan's great gift was his ability to talk about his emotions and about ideas and about religion and about natural things and creatures in terms of physical sensation. He creates in his best work an extraordinary effect of physical effort, sometimes of pain, as though he felt his human limitations as an agony of the body.

This has precious little to do with 'feeling his thought' or the 'unified sensibility'. I am not sure that, by the standards of Donne and Herbert, Vaughan was ever able to think at all. It was, of course, impossible to write this kind of verse without going through the motions of thinking, as Dr Johnson himself suggested. But Vaughan never shows any real power of analysis. He may have been enough of a literary man to follow out certain required patterns; and these *simulated* the processes of thought. But this was a literary not an intellectual procedure. Essentially, Vaughan was a lyric poet; that is, his poetry, as I have said elsewhere, "rises from a single, intense moment of perception and concerns the poet's reaction to the object, rather than the object itself". The label does not describe him exactly. It could never do so, given the literary modes of the time. But it does indicate the area in which Vaughan worked best. When he is most his own man he always manages to convey the effect of a kind of physical equivalent of strong emotion. Where Donne and Herbert created a poetry of direct, personal religious experience, Vaughan extended this until he presented religious feelings as a matter of physical sensation. It is, I think, because the sensations are of their nature fitful that Vaughan's poetry could be at one moment vivid, profound and original, and at the next, dull, prosaic and derivative.

The step beyond Vaughan's best poetry is into a realm where the sensations, aided only by images, do all the work. It is, in fact, the step into Symbolism and, although this style used once to be called Metaphysical poetry, it is a step that was taken by neither Vaughan, nor Donne, nor Herbert, nor any poet of the seventeenth century.

Chapter Four

METAPHYSICAL RHETORIC:
RICHARD CRASHAW

RICHARD CRASHAW is counted a Metaphysical largely by accident. The accident is that he is a writer who worked almost exclusively in terms of conceits and paradoxes, which are techniques now thought to belong only to the Metaphysicals. They do not. But then they are not so insistently used elsewhere in English poetry. So if Crashaw is pushed into the School of Donne it is only because it is difficult to see where else in the English tradition he belongs. He himself encouraged the confusion by calling his most important book of poems *Steps to the Temple*, as a compliment to Herbert. The author of the first preface to the volume—possibly Joseph Beaumont—took good care to point to the link with Herbert, whose poems at that time were highly regarded. Yet even Beaumont can find little similarity beyond the fact that they were both truly devotional poets. Although Crashaw has echoes of Herbert and Donne, they are rarely important and have nothing to do with his unique quality.

There would be no difficulty with Crashaw's poetry if it were not as good as it is. Austin Warren, in his study of the poet, wrote: "Out of a sympathetic study of Southwell and Fletcher, Crashaw could, without question, have acquired the essentials of his final style: the antithesis, the oxymoron, the paradox, alliteration, homoioteleuton; sensuous metaphors for sensuous objects, the sensuous treatment of sacred themes." [1] The elements of Crashaw's style are there in Southwell and Giles Fletcher; he also has qualities in common with Francis Quarles. Yet nobody worries about *them*. At best they are objects of mild scholarly interest; more usually they serve as examples of the quaint. Crashaw is clearly more than that. In fact, there are moments when he sounds like one of the greatest poets in the language:

[1] Austin Warren, *Richard Crashaw, A Study in Baroque Sensibility*, Louisiana State University Press, 1939, p. 117.

73

> Love, thou art absolute sole Lord
> Of life and death. . . .

There are a number of such moments in his verse, when for a line or two, the writing has the power and conviction, control and unmistakably individual movement of major poetry. The trouble is that with Crashaw the major poetry is rarely anything more than momentary. His poetry *is* sustained, but in its own way. And that is not the way of other major English verse. Perhaps this is why the sub-title of Professor Warren's book is *A Study in Baroque Sensibility* and why Professor Mario Praz, in his early study of *Secentismo e Marinismo in Inghilterra*, has called Crashaw the greatest exponent of the Baroque style in any language. For the Baroque was essentially a Continental mode. This is why studies of his work so often end up talking about his relationship to Italian poets. Crashaw was a Continental poet writing in English. He was the forbear not of Hopkins but of Poe.

Compared with the Romance languages English is extraordinarily non-rhetorical. Too many important British writers have said their most profound say in a more or less offhand manner, as though they were improvising at full stretch of the spoken language, heightening and sharpening that, rather than handling a medium that was at all formally apart. Perhaps this has something to do with the fact that the greatest British poet was also a popular dramatist. After all, Milton is our only major poet whose language has very little truck with the colloquial tradition; and he was also the greatest classicist among the poets. Even in Pope, despite all the apparent restriction of the rhymed couplet, a strong current runs between Augustan decorum and what was apparently the conversational tone of the society for which he wrote. In French, on the other hand, there is nearly always a powerful element of formality about artistic utterance. The poets run to abstraction in diction, rules and themes which a certain cadenced solemnity in the language makes sound peculiarly convincing. Hence the *Symbolistes*, who were some of the most intelligent poets who have ever written, admired the pretentious theorizing and empty poetical contraptions of Edgar Allan Poe because he was one of the few poets who ever handled English rather as though it were French. It was as though he wrote in French using English words. The difference between the two traditions is that the French, Italian or Spanish creative intelligence naturally formalizes; it works perfectly and fully through rhetoric. Whereas in English, rhetoric is nearly always a substitute for intelligence.

Crashaw, of course, had nothing to do with any rhetoric of the absolutes, Beauty, Truth and so on, for they were a peculiarly Romantic failing. Crashaw was rhetorical because, more often than not, a minor technical means ran away with the poetic material. His editor, suggesting how the poems can be dated, said that Crashaw's style developed "away from the clearly apprehended imagery and precise metrical forms of his earliest poetry towards a freer verse and more complex metaphorical utterance in which the images, as in Shakespeare's later style, seem to follow each other in quicker succession, without always being clearly conceived or fully exploited". [2] But the difference between Shakespeare's and Crashaw's later use of imagery is vital: Shakespeare's is centripetal, Crashaw's centrifugal. The more Shakespeare adds image to image, the more sharply he defines the feelings which gave rise to them; the more complex he is, the more accurate. Crashaw's images, on the other hand, recede from focus. Imaginative rightness gives way to a perverse logic of ornamentation:

> Water'd by the showres they bring,
> The thornes that thy blest browes encloses
> (A cruell and a costly spring)
> Conceive proud hopes of proving Roses.

This is rhetorical, yet it has nothing to do with the modern rhetoric of imagery, which freewheels round and round the subject without ever quite recognizing it. On the contrary, Crashaw allows each detail to take on too much life and logic of its own. He develops every item to its fullest: blood falls from Christ's wounds like showers; showers come in the spring and because of them plants bloom; since roses have thorns, then thorns in such a red spring might bear roses. Each individual bit has its reasons; how Crashaw arrived at any given line is understandable. The difficulty is not *how* but *why* he arrived there.

This is the difference between Crashaw's conceits and those of Donne or Herbert. The latters' are always firmly related to the real subject of the poems. The poets argue in terms of the conceit on the understanding that what they say is at all points convertible into terms of the personal instance.

[2] *The Poems of Richard Crashaw*, ed. L. C. Martin, Oxford, 1927, pp. xci-xcii.

At the same time, the conceits act as a check to prevent the feelings flying off too high. Donne's conceits are a kind of guarantee that his emotions are discussable in terms of his toughest, most active intellectual interests; Herbert's set off his devotion against the simple objects and interchange of everyday life. The result in both is to ensure their poems of a level of intelligible, common humanity. But the measure of Crashaw's devotion is his inventiveness. His subjects are justified by the ornamentation they can be made to support.

I called Crashaw's imagery centrifugal because, though it is perfectly clear how each image develops ingeniously outwards under its own impetus, it is hard to see how and why the images first arrive. This presumably is what Eliot meant when he charged Crashaw with perversity. He was provoked by this stanza from 'The Teare':

> Faire Drop, why quak'st thou so?
> 'Cause thou streight must lay thy Head
> In the Dust? ô no;
> The Dust shall never bee thy Bed:
> A pillow for thee will I bring,
> Stuft with Downe of Angels wing.

"Crashaw's images," said Mr Eliot, "even when entirely preposterous—for there is no warrant in bringing a pillow (and what a pillow) for the *head* of a *tear*—give a kind of intellectual pleasure—it is a deliberate conscious perversity of language, a perversity like that of the amazing and amazingly impressive interior of St Peter's. There is brain work in it." [3] Mr Eliot is complaining of that constant clash in Crashaw's work between great ingenuity and what appears to be an utter lack of common sense. The clash, certainly, is there. But there is a principle at work behind it. It is less common sense than sense, pure and simple. The criterion of Crashaw's poetry is a matter of, literally, getting the feel of the thing right. An image earns its place if it evokes the apt sensation. For example, in *The Teare* supreme reverence means, for Crashaw, supreme softness and care, a brooding feminine tenderness which is not wholly irrelevant to the poem's subject, Mary Magdalene. Hence that pillow and its stuffing.

The clash, then, in Crashaw's poetry is between an

[3] 'A Note on Richard Crashaw', *For Lancelot Andrewes*, 1928, p. 122.

ornamental logical ingenuity and an overall impressionism. At his extreme he is like a painter working in two styles at once: the dominant structural design is a large impressionist sketch, but the details are picked out with the minutely perverse ingenuity of Hieronimus Bosch.

I am not implying that Crashaw was a kind of clever child of poetry: fundamentally naïve but with a gift for detail. On the contrary, he seems to have had an extraordinarily acute critical habit of mind. He revised his poetry with considerable care and always for the better. And this critical gift worked at every level. He had a sense of relevance: the stanza from 'On the bleeding wounds of our crucified Lord' which I have discussed was omitted from the 1652 version. He had a very sharp eye for effects and, with that, a gift for crystallization. The two versions of his finest poem, the 'Letter to the Countess of Denbigh' (1652 and 1653), show these gifts at their best. The later version is more concentrated and clearly wrought. Yet nothing has been added to the complexity of the poem. Only the order of some of the lines has been changed and the abstractions have been crystallized into detailed images. But by this seemingly insignificant tinkering a great deal has been added to the life and vividness of the work. Crashaw at his best had an objective critical grasp of his own work that is the mark of the highest order of creative intelligence.

By saying, then, that there is a clash between the precise effects and what seem to be imprecise feelings, I am not gainsaying his intelligence, but I am adding something to that epithet 'rhetorical'. Crashaw is the only devotional poet among the Metaphysicals whose devotions, not merely his poetry, are essentially public. Here the converse of 'public' is not 'private' in the modern sense; that is, shut-in and impenetrable. Nor is it just a matter of not writing for publication. Donne, Herbert and Vaughan are not primarily public because they are concerned to record in all fullness the fluctuations of their personal relationships with God. Crashaw's devotional poetry, on the other hand, has to do with the public occasions of religion, with its topics. So he is not concerned with a difficult, subtle inwardness. Instead, once he has caught the appropriate, almost heroic, note of passionate concern, his business is to maintain and amplify it. He is, in a sense, a ritualistic poet. It was not for nothing that he was a convert to the Roman Catholic Church.

A great deal of the adverse criticism of Crashaw's verse centres on the fact that his personal emotions do, in fact, intrude where they shouldn't. For example, he forces the idea of sweetness upon everything he approves of, and the apogee of religious bliss seems to be contained in the word 'nest'. There is at times an over intrusive physical warmth in his dealings with religious subjects that seems out of place. Hence Eliot objected that "we feel at times that his passion for heavenly objects is imperfect because it is partly a substitute for human passion. It is not impure, but it is incomplete"; and Empson did a brilliant analysis of the sexual overtones in the 'Hymn to the Name and Honor of the Admirable Sainte Teresa'. Despite this, Crashaw is not a morbid writer. Though his poetry is sometimes a little indigestible, it is never sickly:

> Vpwards thou dost weep.
> Heaun's bosome drinks the gentle stream.
> Where th'milky riuers creep,
> Thine floates aboue; & is the cream.
> Waters aboue th'Heauns, what they be
> We'are taught best by thy TEARES & thee.

> Euery morn from hence
> A brisk Cherub somthing sippes
> Whose sacred influence
> Addes sweetnes to his sweetest Lippes.
> Then to his musick. And his song
> Tasts of this Breakfast all day long.

This is certainly grotesque. But what is grotesque about it is not so much the detail but the premise from which it springs: the *idea*, pushed to its extreme, that since the Magdalene's weeping was pious it must, therefore, have been upwards towards heaven. But although most of the usual properties of Crashaw's private symbolism are present— bosom, milky rivers, cream, sweetness—the verse is not morbid. More in the lines than the cherub is 'brisk'. There is an element of vigorous enjoyment in the writing itself: in the short clear sentences and the extraordinarily tenacious ingenuity. It is, I think, the public nature of the poem which helps the poet to this full-blooded bravura. His sense of the subject outside himself and of the formal occasion help him maintain his air.

To return to the epithet 'rhetorical': I said that Crashaw is in this more Continental than English because he makes his most powerful and imposing statements through elaborately formal devices. He has, in fact, two of these devices which he uses again and again: the paradox, which is uni-

versal in religious poetry, and a knack of ornamenting to
such a degree that the ornaments take on a lo c—a per-
nic ous life, almost—of their own. For example, his best
known short poem:

> They 'haue let thee naked, LORD, O that they had!
> This garment too I would they had deny'd.
>
> Thee with thy oolf they haue too richly clad;
> Opening the purple wardrobe in thy side.
>
> O neuer could be found garment too good
> For thee to wear, But this, of thine own Blood.

It is a poem based, presumably, on a sense of profound
shock aroused by the sight of 'the Body of our Blessed Lord,
Naked and Bloody'. But there is no attempt at all to present, other than in the title, the scene as it was in itself. Instead, the poet formalizes it wholly into his two devices of
paradox and ornament. In the first four lines these two elements are developed almost independently: in the first and
third lines are the paradoxes (the nakedness which is not
nakedness; the body which has in itself its own clothes); in
the second and fourth is the ornamental corollary of this
paradox. They are connected largely by that trick of the
mind which conceives emotional shock in terms of the intellectual shock of paradox, and that, in turn, in terms of
extreme ingenuity of ornament. Yet there seems to me to
be no trick work at all in the feeling. The poem *is* shocking
and, in an odd way, direct. More so, in fact, than the
stanza of Marino's on which it is based; for that moves more
simply on the conceit that, by sweating blood when he assumed again his heavenly kingdom, Christ was weaving for
himself his royal garments of purple.[4] Without that wardrobe, Marino is altogether smoother and less open to the
charge of lack of taste. But he is also less powerful and concentrated. One could excuse Crashaw's outlandish conceit
in two ways: it may be intended to shock the reader into
that same state of bafflement in which the poet apparently
wrote; or it may suggest the frightening way in which Jesus
allowed himself to be used—his body is reduced to a piece

---

4 Suda sangue (ahi bontade)
  Rè, che prendendo la corona, e'l regno,
  Di rugiadosa porpora celeste
  Tesse a le membra sue la regia veste.
        La Lira, pt. III, p. 190 (ed. 1615).

of common household furniture. Neither, I think, is correct. Crashaw's lines have greater power because their impulse is more of a whole. He was a poet who expressed himself so completely through his techncial devices that extreme passion automatically meant extreme artifice.

It is for this reason I called Crashaw more of a Continental than an English writer. It depends on that word 'artifice'. In English poetry at its best great art-speech is a matter of great control, hence, most often, of great simplicity. Artifice, on the other hand, can exist far more easily *for its own sake,* and in Crashaw's work it often existed without the personal artistic control called 'tact'. He worked instead by the imaginative sweep of public feelings, rather like a heroic poet, and by his extraordinary fecundity of invention. The result was some of the most artificial verse in the language. It has behind it a consistent effort to formalize, distance and elaborate everything, so that no feeling or impression or observed detail ever gets into a poem as itself, only as something else. For instance, one very definite visual image, of 'Our Crucified Lord, Naked and Bloody', has to be translated into another equally definite visual image, that of clothes in a wardrobe—translated, that is, into a man-made article. One can object that the actual scene is not what the poem is really about: what starts it moving is the shock of the *idea* of Christ being naked and bloody; hence like all profound religious emotions it can only be expressed fully in a paradox. Very well. But all the ingenuity has gone into creating a *visual paradox,* a special artificial construction from an idea from an emotion about a scene.

This effort to translate one kind of impression into terms of another was, of course, the essence of Baroque art. This is why the most fruitful scholarly discussion of Crashaw has been in terms of that eminently Continental mode. But it is important to remember that Professor Praz, who is the expert on this, has called Crashaw the major Baroque poet in any language, and has shown in detail how very much better, more original and more alive he was than Marino from whom he apparently borrowed so much. I suggest that it is in his superiority to Marino that Crashaw has most in common with the School of Donne. This is not a sophistry. It is obvious that by a crude interpretation of the conceit, the Metaphysical and Baroque styles do have a certain amount in common. But from that meeting-place one style led off towards what I tentatively called realism, the other towards a more enthusiastic, heroic formulation in terms of an elaborately artificial art. (Incidentally, Thomas Carew probably knew Marino personally, and certainly translated some of his poems and borrowed a number of terms of wit from him; but since he lacked that fundamental enthusiasm, his debt never affected the real tissue of his verse or sensibility.[5]) Simply because Crashaw clearly knew the work of Donne and Herbert well, he was aware of much higher standards of intelligence than ever troubled Marino. Hence the constant but perverse logical pressure in his imagery; hence his critical intelligence about his own work; hence, too, his steady progress towards maturity. The 'Letter to the Countess of Denbigh' is one of his last poems; it is his most perfect and most mature, and it is also, in its flexible, subtle and wide-ranging intelligence, nearest to the style of Donne. This does not make it a jot less original than his Baroque poems. It has the same imaginative power and fecundity. But they are in the service of a personal, intimate intelligence rather than that of what seems to me to be an essentially alien artificiality.

[5] See *The Poems of Thomas Carew*, ed. Rhodes Dunlap, Oxford, 1949, pp. xxxii and lv.

Chapter Five

THE POETRY OF JUDGMENT:
ANDREW MARVELL

IN all the diverse talent of the School of Donne, Richard Crashaw and Andrew Marvell are the two poets most wholly opposed. With Crashaw the recurrent question is why, given that power and fertility, he was not a greater poet. It is as though he had in him the essential stuff of great poetry, but frittered it away. Marvell, on the other hand, produced some of the most perfectly accomplished poems in the language and yet is, for all that, somehow not a 'major poet'. Dr Leavis once wrote of Dryden: "He may be a greater poet than Marvell, but he did not write any poetry as indubitably great as Marvell's best". The corollary is also true: Marvell may have written a few great poems, but he was not a great poet.

He has done very well in this century. Eliot, Leavis and Empson, for example, have been prompted by him to some of their finest criticism. So his excellence is firmly established. I merely want to suggest here why, for all the subtlety and accomplishment of his writing, Marvell was essentially one of the last products of a school, but still too much part of it to be quite able to go forward to the next.

He is, in a way, the School of Donne in miniature, working in all the variations of the style: in 'To his Coy Mistress', 'The Definition of Love' and, in another way, 'On a Drop of Dew', he writes like Donne; in 'The Cornet' and 'Eyes and Tears' he is largely a follower of Herbert; 'The Fair Singer' and 'The Picture of Little T. C.' are like Carew and Lovelace; 'Upon Appleton House' is heavily influenced by Cleveland; 'A Dialogue between the Resolved Soul and Created Pleasure' has something of the formal stance of Cowley; his pastoral poems have behind them an Elizabethan and Continental tradition which descended through poets like Aurelian Townshend; 'The Nymph complaining for the death of her Faun' sounds like a kind of pastoral-classical Crashaw; he went on to write political satires in rhymed couplets. In none of these poems was he a mere imitator; he always rehandled his themes and styles in a peculiarly original way. But the variety and varied perfection of his work show that, despite his correct, almost sedate, career—gentleman tutor, government official, M.P.—he was, purely in terms of technical accomplishment, one of the most professional of that extraordinary group of amateurs that made up the School of Donne. He was, in short, the most 'literary', while Crashaw, with his religious-heroic style, his inventive enthusiasm and his Baroque principle of sensuous substitution, was the most 'rhetorical' The difference is between a poet whose intelligence worked *on* literature, critically and analytically, and a poet who needed a great deal of artifice in order to express his intelligence at all.

The main element in Marvell's poetry is its balance, its pervading sense of intelligent proportion. He is, I think, the foremost poet of judgment in the English language, and 'An Horatian Ode' is his foremost poem. By *judgment* I mean a quality which presents, balances and evaluates a whole situation, seeing all the implications and never attempting to simplify them. The poet's whole effort is directed towards a full and delicate sanity, so that what he finally achieves is a kind of personal impersonality. For example:

> 'Tis Madness to resist or blame
> The force of angry Heavens flame:
> And, if we would speak true,
> Much to the Man is due.

The poem gets its effect by the certainty with which it balances the large religious and political context—in the first couplet—against a personal judgment, so that both appear necessary parts of a whole understanding of the situation. Again:

> . . .(Who) Could by industrious valour climbe
> To ruine the great Work of Time,
> And cast the Kingdome old
> Into another Mold.
> Though Justice against Fate complain,
> And plead the Antient Rights in vain:
> But those who do hold or break
> As Men are strong or weak.
> Nature that hateth emptiness,
> Allows of penetration less:
> And therefore must make room
> Where greater Spirits come.

I have seen the lines used as an example of political slipperiness, as though Marvell were praising Cromwell whilst fundamentally supporting the king. But what in fact is so impressive in the poem is the sureness with which the poet separates out the various threads so that he can proceed without disorder in the full knowledge of what his feelings on the subject really are. Personal preferences and natural sanity hold each other in check. His distaste for that kind of hard-working ambition, particularly when it sets itself up against the tested sanctities of tradition, sway the balance one way. His acknowledgment of the natural and rational laws of power sway it back the other. This manner of opposing two ways of thinking and feeling is, of course, typical of a good deal of Metaphysical poetry. But elsewhere—in, say, Herbert's 'The Collar' or 'Affliction (I)'—the turnabout always follows some peculiarly intricate dialectic by which the poet argues himself into accepting his full responsibilities. He presents the whole process of understanding: the knot, the gradual untying and the final ordering of the threads. In Marvell's poetry, on the other hand, the personal balance is already achieved before the poem begins. He approaches his subjects fully aware of his personal bias. The result is that he always has the air of a man dealing with something outside him, rather than with what at least began as an unresolved complex of emotions. It is this impression of the mind detachedly at play over a number of possible choices that earns Marvell the title of poet of judgment. Another way of putting it would be to call him a political poet. Certainly, 'An Horatian Ode' is one of the two finest political poems in the language; the other is *Coriolanus*. As a political poet he works analytically, resolving at every point personal choice into a larger context of general or social responsibilities. In this sense, Marvell is closer to Dryden and Pope than he is to Donne.

This habit of always leaving himself the elbow-room of impersonality—whether it is called judgment, a political trick of the mind, or a peculiar intensity of civilization—has saved him from the excesses of his interpreters. There is, for example, an aura of suggestiveness about a great deal of his work that can, with a little effort, be translated into symbolism of a kind. But the fact that Marvell disliked violence—which we know from comments not in his poems—appreciated the peace and quiet of gardens as a relief from the turbulence of the Civil War, and so wrote eloquently, in one disguise or another, on the subject of Eden, does not make him a Quietist, nor does it illuminate his poetry with flashes of mystical insight *à propos* of God or Nature. The strangeness of a poem like 'The Nymph complaining for the death of her Faun', or of that unexpected couplet in 'Bermudas':

> But Apples plants of such a price,
> No Tree could ever bear them twice.

is no evidence of any specific, extendable religious symbolism in Marvell's verse, nor of any plan to take his readers in by writing charmingly about what was really very serious. Marvell's use of religion seems to be much the same as his classicism. The subtlety of some of the nymph's complaints for her faun:

> Had it liv'd long, it would have been
> Lillies without, Roses within.

or

> There is not such another in
> The World, to offer for their Sin.

is neither greater nor less than that of:

> The brotherless *Heliades*
> Melt in such Amber Tears as these.

Empson once wrote of this last couplet: "It is tactful, when making an obscure reference, to arrange that the verse should be intelligible even when the reference is not understood. . . . If you had forgotten, as I had myself, who their brother was, and look it up, the poetry will scarcely seem more beautiful; such of the myth as is wanted is implied." [1] The Biblical echoes are tantalizing and evocative in precisely the same way: they lend the poem weight and seriousness. But they do not restrict the area of its action to their own special realm. The Bible came more naturally to the seventeenth century than to our day; it did not demand any peculiarly specialized effort of attention. For Marvell, as for every other educated man of his time, the Bible, like the classics, was a dimension of his extraordinarily civilized sensibility, and was controlled by it.

It is this that makes him such a deliberate, literary and

---

[1] *Seven Types of Ambiguity*, 1947, p. 167.

decorous poet, particularly in his conceits. *Pace* Eliot, I cannot see that Marvell was ever carried away by his in-genuity with metaphors. But he came, as I said, at the end of the School of Donne and so could judge the technical means both for its vitality and in its corruption. And the corrupt conceit had effects very different from Donne's. In short, Marvell had read and taken good account of Cleve-land; which meant he knew how to play the game of wit when it suited him. It was this element that Eliot missed when he accused Marvell's figure of the 'Antipodes in shoes' of being one of those "images which are over-developed or distracting; which support nothing but their own mis-shapen bodies".[2] There is a side to Marvell's wit less serious than the one Eliot wished to emphasize. You can see it directly the conceit is put in its full context:

> But now the *Salmon-Fisher's* moist
> Their *Leathern Boats* begin to hoist;
> And, like *Antipodes* in Shoes,
> Have shod their *Heads* in their *Canoos*.
> How *Tortoise* like, but not so slow,
> These rational *Amphibii* go?
> Let's in: for the dark *Hemisphere*
> Does now like one of them appear.

Marvell's concept of wit was flexible enough to include the kind of deliberate playfulness that is found now only in light verse, and, if Eliot's *Old Possum* poems are typical, not often in that. The 'Antipodes in shoes', in fact, is not so much a conceit as a joke. And Marvell works for it de-liberately. There is a preparatory pun in the preceding line: 'Leathern Boats' suggests 'boots' and so makes way for the 'shoes'; a solemn pedantry in the couplet following, and a final piece of absurdity—the comparison of the dark com-ing down over the hemisphere with the coracles over the heads of the fishermen. They all have the same effect, and the effect is deliberately comic. 'Deliberately', since it is unlikely that a poet as skilful as Marvell would have lapsed so grotesquely at the end of a long poem without knowing why. I suggest he has two reasons: the first has to do with the occasion of the poem, the second with its literary means.

The absurd solemnity of that closing stanza may be more extreme than anything that has gone before in the poem but it is the same in kind. The poem is dedicated to Lord

2 'Andrew Marvell', *Selected Essays*, 1951, p. 297.

Fairfax, whose child, Mary, Marvell was then tutoring. All through the poem Marvell has treated the conventional occasions for conventionally exaggerated praise with a polite mock-seriousness, using conceits that are too conceited, too extreme. This does not hinder him from being very serious indeed in praising what he really admires in Fairfax, the political moderation and the firm desire for peace. But he writes with such delicate control that he can change from the fanciful to the profound without any clashing of gears. The whole effort presumes on a kind of formal intimacy between the poet and his audience: Marvell can be witty with his conventional praise because it is understood that his patron has qualities rarer and finer. In that sense it is a family poem; it would not be in good taste to be fulsome where fulsomeness is to be expected from everyone.

It is also a family poem in that the fancy is supposed to be amusing. And not only, I suggest, to Lord Fairfax. Compare, for example, those infamous 'Antipodes' with a far more successful passage:

> And now to the Abbyss I pass
> Of that unfathomable Grass,
> Where Men like Grashoppers appear,
> But Grashoppers are Gyants there:
> They, in their squeking Laugh, contemn
> Us as we walk more low then them:
> And, from the Precipices tall
> Of the green spir's, to us do call.

This is a conceit, but it is hardly Metaphysical. It is, instead, nearer the wit of Lewis Carroll. The conceit, that is, is a matter of sharply re-focusing the scene until it is adjusted to a child's vision: the hay tall enough to drown in and the grasshoppers gigantic, threatening presences. There was nothing in the detached elegance of the wit at Marvell's command which barred him from writing vivid, adult poetry which might also amuse a child. The tradition of an exclusively patronizing children's verse did not seem to have existed in the seventeenth century; perhaps it did not begin until Isaac Watts stooped to conquer. Marvell's conceit is no less successful because, like the elaborate pedantry of the 'Antipodes in shoes', it has behind it a faint nonsense air.

I am far from accusing Marvell of quaintness or suggesting that his poetry was, in any way, kid's stuff. On the contrary, Marvell's ability to blend this kind of fanciful exaggeration with a far more serious wit, and to give both an equivalent, if not an equal, subtlety, is a measure of his sophistication. It is pre-eminently a literary sophistication. Far from being victimized by the style, the poet seems perfectly aware of what the exaggerated conceit is and is not good for. It is, in fact, possible that by using this kind of witty playfulness to amuse the daughter of the house he is even taking the measure of the corrupt Metaphysical style. The most elaborate conceits begin when Mary Fairfax enters the poem, and this coincides with an obvious and deliberate echo of Cleveland. Marvell has:

> See how the Flow'rs, as at *Parade,*
> Under their *Colours* stand displaid:
> Each *Regiment* in order grows,
> That of the Tulip Pinke and Rose. . . .

Cleveland wrote:

> The trees, like yeomen of her guard,
> Serving more for pomp than ward,
> Ranked on each side, with loyal duty
> Weave branches to enclose her beauty. . . .

I am not pretending that Marvell's poem is really an elaborate critical parody of Cleveland; but it does seem that when he played Cleveland's game of wit to amuse his patron and his pupil, he was showing that he knew its precise range and value. Instead of being occasionally the victim of false wit, Marvell used it for his own ends.

I have defended at length some not very distinguished lines in order to point up a vital aspect of the poetry of judgment: its peculiarly literary control in the choice and manipulation of special styles for special effects. If these are an index of poetic achievement, then Marvell is a master. But when compared with Donne, it seems that what Marvell gained in control he lost in pressure. He rarely, if at all, lapses as Donne did at times. But then he hasn't the excuse. He was never as original; his poetic discoveries were within already charted poetic forms. His first desire in verse was, I think, to do it perfectly. And he gained this perfection by keeping away from insistently personal situations and absorbing all his energies in the literary form and process. He rarely has that air of creative improvisation, of having to invent a new form for a unique occasion. Instead, each poem seems to start from a peculiarly sensitive critical analysis of the particular genre.

Consider, for instance, 'The Definition of Love':

> My Love is of a birth as rare
> As 'tis for object strange and high:
> It was begotten by despair
> Upon Impossibility.
>
> Magnanimous Despair alone
> Could show me so divine a thing,
> Where feeble Hope could ne'r have flown
> But vainly flapt its Tinsel Wing.
>
> And yet I quickly might arrive
> Where my extended Soul is fixt,
> But Fate does Iron wedges drive,
> And alwaies crouds it self betwixt.
>
> For Fate with jealous Eye doth see
> Two perfect Loves; nor lets them close:
> Their unione would her ruine be,
> And her Tyrannick pow'r depose.
>
> And therefore her Decrees of Steel
> Us as the distant Poles have plac'd,
> (Though Loves whole World on us doth wheel)
> Not by themselves to be embrac'd.
>
> Unless the giddy Heaven fall,
> And Earth some new Convulsion tear;
> And, us to joyn, the World should all
> Be cramp'd into a *Planisphere*.
>
> As Lines so Loves *oblique* may well
> Themselves in every Angle greet;
> But ours so truly *Paralel*,
> Though infinite can never meet.
>
> Therefore the Love which us doth bind,
> But Fate so enviously debarrs,
> Is the Conjunction of the Mind,
> And Opposition of the Stars.

It is based on a single aspect of some of Donne's love poems: his habit of bolstering up a feeling with abstract and scientific imagery until it can bear the weight of his complex logic. But Marvell presses this logical abstraction so hard that the feeling which justifies it seems to refine away to nothing. This is apparent in the imagery. The poem begins with three-dimensional allegorical figures—Despair, Hope, Fate—with tinsel wings, iron wedges and decrees of steel, who control 'Loves *whole* World'. It is all hard, solid and definite. The substantial globe, however, is then reduced to a two-dimensional model, the planisphere, and that, in turn, is reduced to the mere lines of a geometrical figure. Marvell's conclusion about the abstract refinement of their love—'the Conjunction of the Mind'—is borne out by the steady abstraction of the imagery. The poem is less of a love poem than an essay in abstraction. The poet, presumably, meant something of this kind when he called it 'The Definition of Love'. He is not to be criticized for failing to write a poem he never intended. But perhaps the piece is more formally perfect and neat than most of Donne's because Marvell has only the formal aspects to bother about. His stake in the thing seems first and foremost craftsmanly.

Marvell's practice in 'The Definition of Love' is the rule for his work, not the exception. There is not one of his love poems which, when set next to any of Donne's, seems more than an exercise in the poetic kind. This holds even for one of his most perfect poems, 'To his Coy Mistress'. I cannot believe that, in terms of the poem—the biography, in these matters, being neither here nor there—the mistress ever existed. She is merely part of the poem's traditional occasion. She is of course wooed with wit and some admirable ironical flourishes. But the irony is largely at Marvell's own expense:

> Thou by the *Indian Ganges* side
> Should'st Rubies find: I by the Tide
> Of *Humber* would complain. . . .

She is to do exotic things in exotic surroundings, while he is left to scribble away at his complaints on the dreary banks of the Humber, which flows through his native city, Hull. Even the brilliant conceit of his 'vegetable love' gains an extra dimension of irony when you remember his 'green thought in a green shade' and all those innocent, Eden-like gardens to which Marvell wrote so many love poems of another kind. As for his mistress and his ideal love-making:

> An hundred years should go to praise
> Thine Eyes, and on thy Forehead Gaze ... etc.

That, as the editors have pointed out, is founded on a turn
of wit that Marvell took from Cowley. But the tone of the
verse deepens and the rhythm becomes more charged when,
in the section beginning "But at my back I alwaies hear ..."
the subject changes from the girl to death. It is this sudden
quickening of the witty detachment into something distinctly more sharply felt that makes me certain that Marvell is addressing himself rather than any supposed mistress.
The real and moving poem is about time, death, waste and
the *need* to love, rather than about love itself. Whatever of
its power does not come from this source comes from the
perfection of the performance: from the inevitable syllogistic
progression (by which, incidentally, Marvell argues himself
into accepting images of violence and war that go flatly
against the current of all his other poetry), and, as Eliot
said, from the weight behind the verse of the whole tradition
of European love poetry.

One of the main differences between Marvell and Donne
was not in the sophistication of their wit, which was where
most of the other late Metaphysicals fell down, but in the
uses their wit was put to. Donne's was exploratory; it
brought whole and unexpected areas of awareness into the
service of his single, immediate situation; and in doing so
he changed the whole language of poetry. By accommodating it to the extraordinary range of his intelligence and to
the kind of sceptical intensity of feeling of which he was
master, he introduced into poetry a wholly new standard
of realism. Marvell's wit, on the other hand, worked in
literary forms already to hand and perfected them; it was
a force that restrained, controlled and impersonalized.

But there are moments, admittedly rare, when this emphasis on civilized control and artistic impersonality lapses
into what might, in a poet less skilled, be vulgar indifference:

> How wide they dream! The *Indian* Slaves,
> That sink for Pearl through Seas profound,
> Would find her Tears yet deeper Waves
> And not of one the bottom sound.
>
> I yet my silent Judgment keep,
> Disputing not what they believe:
> But sure as oft as Women weep,
> It is to be suppos'd they grieve.

The first stanza is one of the most allusive Marvell ever wrote, and he always wrote well on tears. Rhythmically, I think, it is based on Donne:

> O wrangling schooles, that search what fire
> Shall burne this world, had none the wit
> Unto this knowledge to aspire,
> That this her feaver might be it?

But Marvell's stanza has undergone a distancing typical of his work; it is something more than merely changing 'wrangling' to 'dreaming'. The slight roughness of Donne's verse has wholly disappeared: for example, the repetition of 'that' and 'this' so close together, which gives the lines their colloquial directness and which depends on the personal cadence of the speaking voice to carry them off. Gone, too, is the reference to a lively contemporary issue—the Schoolmen at that time were very much under attack. The essence of Marvell's conceit is a certain exotic quality; he uses all the technical skill he can muster to build up the strangeness and grandeur of the weeping woman: the alliteration of consonants and vowels, for example, which makes the second and third lines echo on themselves. But having built up his effects with such imaginative strength, Marvell seems able to reassert his 'silent Judgment' only by a final gesture of lame cynicism. Admittedly, the last stanza is more in keeping with the tone of the rest of the poem than is that oddly rich conceit. But the renewed cynicism is so sudden and extreme that it makes me suspect that that beautiful detachment of Marvell's was, at times, defensive. If Donne is also guilty at times of sudden lapses into cynicism the occasions are always a matter of too much assertion, never of too delicate a withdrawal.

With the exception of George Herbert, Marvell is the most considerable of Donne's followers. But his strength is quite different. He is, as I suggested, far more carefully and absorbedly a craftsman in poetry; and this went with a different poetic stance. It matters not a jot that his love poems are thin in comparison with Donne's; there is, after all, little outside Shakespeare's sonnets that can stand that comparison. The difference is between kinds of poets: between the poet whose first concern is to judge and the poet who, above all, synthesizes. The vitality of Donne's poetry depends on his knack of taking on everything that comes with the same immediacy, accuracy and full, tough intelligence. At the end of any of Donne's poems the forces have been resolved and ordered in such a way as to make you believe that a similar readjustment of the feelings has taken place in the poet himself. It is, in a sense, a poetry of action. Marvell, however, is always a little further outside his subjects. His extraordinarily civilized sophistication is a fixed quantity. With it he weighs and judges his material with such dispassionate fairness as to leave you, as a final and lasting taste, with the mature subtlety of his judgment. Unlike Donne and Herbert, he never writes a poem which shows him in the process of attaining this maturity. It is, rather, a quality without which he would not have been able to begin to write. Marvell's detached and sophisticated wit may be infinitely more subtle and less stereotyped than that of the Augustan Man of Sense, but it is of essentially the same kind. In achievement, if not chronologically, he is the last of the School of Donne.

Chapter Six

THE GAME OF WIT AND THE
CORRUPTION OF THE STYLE

I BEGAN by trying to define Donne's style in terms of the intellectual tone and preoccupations of his intimate group. I suggested that his main endeavour was to put over his exceptionally wide-ranging and agile intelligence with as little fuss and as much realism as possible. Though this meant avoiding at all costs the conventionally poetical, it needed a great deal of technical skill and originality to do so without appearing, like most of the other members of his group, flat and tiresome. The power and immediacy of Donne's achievement somehow, I also suggested, altered the language of poetry. He introduced two new rhythms: the rhythm of the colloquial, speaking voice, and the rhythm of what had best be called the intelligence—since I can think of no other word for the habitual mixture of feeling and thought. On these two rhythms was based his realism, which was in sharp contrast with the more conventional Elizabethan poets' habit of translating everything into a glowing but remote and almost abstract world of specialized poetic experience. The work of Donne and his followers was, of course, also highly specialized and skilled, but the whole technical effort was to appear not so. I then tried to show how his followers extended and varied Donne's discoveries for their own needs. The result was the richest body of personal poetry in the language. But it has in common a certain quality of poetic realism rather than any particular technical processes: not the conceit, nor harshness, nor obscurity, but the sharpness of dramatized experience and the complexity of thinking about it.

How and where, then, did it go wrong? For it clearly did go wrong. When the Restoration critics, headed by Dryden, attacked the School of Donne, and when Dr Johnson a hundred-odd years later finished it off, they had plenty of bad verse to support them. Yet it was not the educated professional men of Donne's original circle, nor the writers of devotional poetry, nor the courtiers who, in the bad sense, 'affected the metaphysics'. The degradation of Donne's monarchy of wit was brought about by men who most prided themselves on their command of it: the academics, such as Cleveland, John Hall and Samuel Austin, and private gentlemen with academic yearnings, like Benlowes, and London hacks like Robert Wild. The courtiers may have made their wit into something rather more formal and elegant than Donne's, but it was the academics who reduced it to a formula, the purpose of which was, as Dr Johnson said, 'to show their learning'. They were not professional poets, but they were professionally learned and they often tried, it appears, to be professionally witty. In a way, they resembled Donne's original imitators: worthless, vanished poets like Cornwallis and Roe; they were determined to ape the style in order to appropriate for themselves the title of wit. But Cleveland and the others had one advantage: they were further removed from Donne in time. So it was easier for them to analyse his wit in cold blood. They could recognize the necessary technical procedures and produce their necessary formula.

The formula was for the 'strong line'. This, as it happens, was by no means Cleveland's invention. The ingredients for it are in Donne; the phrase was first used in print as early as 1621 and there are signs that it was used in the Universities before that.[1] But the degenerate strong lines that drew all the attacks were Cleveland's doing. I mentioned earlier that there was a traditional distinction between "the masculine and refined pleasures of the understanding . . . (and) the feminine and sensual of the eye" (Benlowes's words again).[2] If you look at the tributes to Donne you will find that almost everyone in some way or other commented on his 'masculinity'. Carew's 'Elegie' is founded on the idea and Donne himself described his own verse that way a number of times. The word went automatically with being a wit—a man and a poet of intellect. So the strong line was, as it were, the unit of masculine poetry. In both writing and understanding it the intellect counted for more than the ear; hence, too, the cult of harshness that went along with this style. All this was perfectly traditional. But the odd thing

[1] See George Williamson, 'Strong Lines', *English Studies*, XVIII, 1936, pp. 152-9, and *The Senecan Amble*, 1951, pp. 195-9.

[2] R. L. Sharp in *From Donne to Dryden*, Chapel Hill, 1940, pp. 49-53, and in 'Some Light on Metaphysical Obscurity and Roughness', *Studies in Philology*, XXXI, 1934, p. 497ff, has amassed a good deal of material on this. But see Rosemond Tuve in *Elizabethan and Metaphysical Imagery*, Chicago, 1947, p. 136, footnote, and pp. 139-40.

about the word 'masculine' is that it will not be limited to traditional distinctions. From Donne to Coleridge to the present day, the word has always been qualified so as to imply precisely the marks of excellence fashionable at the particular moment. Hence when Donne speaks of "my words masculine perswasive force" (in 'Elegie XVI') and Carew of Donne's "line of masculine expression" and "imperious wit", they are both implying something more than merely the intellectual. For Donne's work is masculine in the more usual sense; it is rigorous, independent and sane, which is the tone of the narrator of 'Satyre I':

> But Oh, God strengthen thee, why stoopest thou so?
> Why? he hath travayld; Long? No; but to me
> (Which understand none) he doth seeme to be
> Perfect French, and Italian; I replyed,
> So is the Poxe. . . .

In this tough, witty voice Donne made his objections to the indignities of 'whining Poetry'. But there was also a further overtone to 'masculine': that is, 'active'. This meant something more than just getting things done and said in poetry. It also implied a whole world of responsibility both to the writer himself and to his position in society. Donne once wrote a magnificent letter to Sir Henry Goodyer on this subject:

> I would not that death should take me asleep. I would not have him meerly seise me, and onely declare me to be dead, but win me, and overcome me. When I must shipwrack, I would do it in a Sea, where mine impotencie might have some excuse; not in a sullen weedy lake, where I could not have so much as exercise for my swimming. Therefore I would fain do something; but that I cannot tell what is no wonder. For to chuse, is to do: but to be no part of any body, is to be nothing.[3]

This was written during the period of his disgrace, when he was unemployed, child-ridden and in danger of being patronized merely as a poet. The letter makes wonderfully clear that vibration behind all his verse: his desire for fulfilment within the body of society as an active, intelligent, professionally trained man. This is why he objected so strongly to being known as a poet: from this masculine point of

[3] *Letters to Severall Persons of Honour*, 1651, p. 44.

view a poet was somehow parasitic, a mere entertainer who did not fulfil any serious function. His emphasis on the active and professional intelligence in some way affects the whole tone of his poetry. It goes with his insistence on a rigorous pattern. Together they give his poems a strong sense of purpose. By the end of every poem something new has been stated, proved, resolved. Part of Donne's strength, in short, and part of his 'masculinity' lies in the way he always manages to give his experience an overall sense of structure.

It is precisely this scope and dialectical sense of purpose that Cleveland's strong lines lack. Fundamentally, Cleveland was a writer of epigrams.[4] His aim was always compression, the greatest amount of sense and allusion in the fewest possible words. He took over from Donne his point-making flair but dispensed with the machinery that justified it. He dispensed, too, with the situations, for the poetry of Cleveland and his followers is sharply distinguished from the rest of the School of Donne in being utterly undramatic. It is, instead, in both situations and reference, verbal. The only personal pressure behind Cleveland's verse is his desire to be clever with words; his subjects are merely excuses for this. Consequently, his renowned compression is not the result of bringing together and harmonizing the conflicting variety of experience but of exploiting the possibilities of words. "Clevelandism", for Dryden, was "wresting and torturing a word into another meaning."[5] And the more Clevelandism degenerated, the more violent the wresting and torturing became. The nadir of the whole movement is the slim volume by Samuel Austin the younger, called *Naps Upon Parnassus. A Sleepy Muse nipt and pincht, though not awakened* (1658). It is a peculiarly unfunny University joke at the expense of a fashion. But the mock tributes and letters before Mr Austin's efforts, though cumbersome, have a useful irony which shows how far the movement went in obscurity and punning:

> In the whole *series* of your Letter, I finde a greate many *Metaphors*, things, which some count *Absolute;* but I tell you they are Obsolete, and to advise you by all means not to *love* them, but to *leave* them; I would have you take a *word,* and *Twang* it; then *listen how*

[4] See W. Lee Ustick and Hoyt H. Hudson, 'Wit, "Mixt Wit", and the Bee in Amber', *Huntington Library Bulletin,* VIII, 1935, pp. 103-30.

[5] 'An Essay of Dramatic Poesy,' 1668, *Essays of John Dryden,* ed. W. P. Ker, 2 vols. Oxford, 1900, I, p. 31.

it sounds; observe diligently its *Reverberation,* mark its *Eccho,* and if *that* chance to bring into your minde any other *Consonant word, apprehend* it be sure, in spite of all the repugnancy which a *dissonant Vowel,* or two may make. Take but this *Course,* and you shall have all my Blessing, and none of my curse.[6]

The anonymous writer of this hasn't got the trick quite right. Neither Austin nor his master, Cleveland, ever punned with the abandon of Lyly or even of Shakespeare, out of verbal exhilaration. Benlowes came closest to that with his:

Death is a noun, yet not declin'd in any case.

This is better than anything Cleveland ever managed; indeed, the next poet to muster that kind of verbal ingenuity was William Empson.[7] In Cleveland's verse, however, and in the verse of all his followers—including, as it happens, most of Benlowes's—the pun becomes the logic, or the guiding principle, of his conceits. For example, the most grotesque of all conceits, Austin's 'Upon my Mother's running Eyes':

. . . my *Pen,* which in your brine I sop,
Which *Dripping bast's* your *raw cheeks* while they drop.

The fact that tears drip and dripping is used in cooking is reason enough to develop the conceit. That it reduces his mother's tears to grease and her cheeks to raw meat does not deter the poet in the least. The pun justifies everything. Cleveland is much the same, though usually less extreme:

No rosary this vot'ress needs—
Her very syllables are beads;
No sooner 'twixt those rubies born,
But jewels are in ear-rings worn.

Cleveland's method here is to take the common stock of amatory metaphors—the mistress as a votaress of love, her

---

[6] 'Answer to (Author's) Epistle (to the University of Cambridge)', C8.

[7] Benlowes, in fact, has his moments when he seems to have forestalled the Empson note:
Garnish no Bristows with rich mine,
Glow-worms are vermin, tho' they shine.
Cf.   Crash is a cloth but poisons are all greens.

lips as rubies, etc.—and link them by a kind of punning on metaphors. One metaphor suggests the next; that suggests yet another; and so on. It is more visual than aural. The only strict pun in the lines is the one that clinches them, the 'ear-rings'. That holds together the jewels, the inner shape of the ear (like Marvell's 'deaf with the drumming of an ear') and the ordinary, necessary act in which these came together, hearing.

The ingenuity is at full stretch in Cleveland's verse *not* in yoking heterogeneous ideas by violence together but simply in joining up as many ideas and images as possible, heterogeneous or not, by their accidents of sound and sight. The process is far more casual than Dr Johnson implied, more a game of word-association than a formal method.

This is what Hobbes meant when he attacked "the ambitious obscurity of expressing more then is perfectly conceived, or perfect conception in fewer words then it requires. Which Expressions, though they have had the honor to be called strong lines, are indeed no better then Riddles."[8] Hobbes had no objection to far-fetched images (this comes, after all, from his commendation of Davenant's *Gondibert*): "From *Knowing much*," he said, "proceedeth the admirable variety and novelty of Metaphors and Similitudes, which are not possible to be lighted on in the compass of a narrow knowledge". His objection is to lack of an ulterior poetic motive, to compression merely for the sake of compression, ingenuity for ingenuity's sake. He objects to the degenerate strong lines, not to the masculine style.

Hobbes also held strong views on language, particularly on what he called "the affectation of words newly brought home from travail", or "words of Art, though of use in the Schools".[9] And these, more even than conceited metaphors, were the basis of Cleveland's strong lines. I said he had a formula for them and have implied that it was a formula for compression and obscurity. The conceit which it used most was one of technical terms, a play with and on learning. It is this that gives all his strong lines the same ring and the same kind of reference:

> ". . . whose fate we see
> Thus copied out in grief's hydrography"

8 'Answer to Davenant', 1650, *Critical Essays of the Seventeenth Century*, ed. J. E. Spingarn, Oxford, 1908, 3 vols., II, p. 63.
9 *Idem*, p. 65, and 'The Virtues of an Heroic Poem', 1675, Spingarn II, p. 68.

". . . alone he is
The Purlieu of a metampsychosis"

"Without the tincture of tautology"

"O the accursed stenography of fate!"

"It is the rose that bleeds, when he
Nibbles his nice phlebotomy"

"There's nothing lives; life is, since he is gone,
But a nocturnal lucubration"

"She, she it is that doth contain all bliss,
And makes the world but her periphrasis"

These are merely some of the prizes of the collection; Cleveland's verse is full of similar lines. And the last two show where his formula came from: not from Donne's *Songs and Sonets,* nor from his *Divine Poems,* but from the *Anniversaries.* This, for example, from the first of them:

Shee, who by making full perfection grow,
Peeces a Circle, and still keepes it so,
Long'd for, and longing for it, to heaven is gone,
Where shee receives, and gives addition . . .

The Anniversaries were Donne's most learned, most abstractly metaphysical and most conceited poems. They were also his most controversial [10] and, because they were almost the only works of his to be published during his lifetime, they were also the most infamously public. They were, in short, a natural source for a University man with a good deal of pedantry in him and a great desire to show off his learning and wit.

At no point, however, are Cleveland's abstractions sustained. This, indeed, accounts for his popularity and influence. He evolved a formula which gave, to paraphrase Mr Jorrocks, all the pleasures of metaphysics and only five

[10] Ben Jonson told William Drummond of Hawthornden "That Dones Anniversarie was profane and full of Blasphemies. That he told Mr Done, if it had been written of ye Virgin Marie it had been something to which he answered that he described the Idea of a Woman and not as she was." *Conversations with William Drummond of Hawthornden* 1619, *Ben Jonson,* ed. C. H. Herford and Percy Simpson, Oxford, 1925-52, 11 vols., I, p. 133.

and twenty per cent. of the danger. This formula for the strong line, which could be applied for certain effects, no matter what the writer's usual habits and style, was used constantly in mid-century verse. Benlowes's poems are full of quasi-philosophic polysyllables, such as these directions to his Fancy on the style of *Theophila*:

> Cull metaphors well-weigh'd and clear,
> Enucleate mysteries to th'ear.
> Be wit stenographied, yet free;
> 'Tis largest in epitome.
> Fly through *Art's* heptarchy, be clad
> With wings to soar, but not to gad.

Benlowes, of course, was Cleveland's most devoted imitator. Yet even a poet like Lovelace, for all his courtly polish, pads his epigrammatic poems in the same way:

> Compendious snail! thou seem'st to me
> Large Euclid's strict epitome.

The same formula is found in a quite different poet, William Chamberlayne, a country doctor, who wrote the epic *Pharonnida*:

> . . . His name must be
> Contracted into that stenography.[11]

and he rose at least to one excellent Cleveland-like conceit:

> Dare curse their new discoveries which placed in
> Hell's geography Americas of sin.

11 Since this comes from *Pharonnida*, Book I, canto IV, ll. 221-2, Chamberlayne may not have read Cleveland when he wrote it. He had reached the end of Book II of *Pharonnida* by the time of the second battle of Newbury in October 1644 (see *Minor Poets of the Caroline Period*, ed. George Saintsbury, Oxford, 1905, 3 vols, I, p. 6.) and Cleveland's *Poems* did not appear until 1647. But Cleveland's poem 'On the memory of Mr Edward King' had appeared in 1638, along with 'Lycidas' and others. On the other hand, Chamberlayne may have got his strong lines straight from Donne, whom he had certainly read. In *Pharonnida*, Book II, canto I, ll. 161 ff., he plagiarized 'The Flea':

> Sudden and *cruel* was the act; yet stands
> Not treason here; but whilst their *purpled* hands
> Yet reeked in *blood*, their *guilty* souls to stain . . .

Cf.   *Cruell* and *Sodaine*, hast thou since
> *Purpled* thy nail, in *blood* of innocence?
> Wherein could this flea *guilty* bee . . .

These three poets are merely a cross-section of the varied dabblers who used the formula. It is rare for a minor writer in the second quarter of the seventeenth century not to have a strong line or two embedded somewhere in his work, whatever the school he belonged to.

Cleveland's strong lines were degenerate because they were nothing more than a linguistic trick to give the appearance of learning without ever sustaining or even needing it. The polysyllabics are essentially ornamental, more elaborate and difficult than whatever the poet really had to say. Like the curlicues of Victorian Gothic, they are there both to cover up the basic lack of design and to make it somehow richer and stranger. As ornaments, however, they are anything but elegant. So the pleasure they gave was presumably the coterie pleasure of recognition. And that, I suggested, was one of the initial pleasures of Donne's verse. The difference is that, for the latter, learning was not all-important. It was, instead, a common background, something easily assumed, that went with the scepticism and the dialectical toughness. In short, it was merely a necessary dimension in which the full intelligence could work. Cleveland's strong lines, on the other hand, were much more deliberately a way of flattering his readers into the belief that, if they could pick up the references and translate the terms, they had won their way into an exclusive coterie of wits and learned gentlemen. Yet this coterie was not quite as select as it now appears, for Cleveland was a publishing, popular poet, whose strong lines were stuffed with the easily recognized technical vocabulary of the Universities. John Evelyn pointed this out in a letter of 1665 to Sir Peter Wyche, the Chairman of the Royal Society's Committee 'for improving the English tongue':

> . . . there are some elegant words introduc'd by physitians chiefly and philosophers, worthy to be retained; others, it may be, fitter to be abrogated; since there ought to be a law as well as a liberty in this particular. And in this choyce there would be some reguard had to the well sounding and more harmonious words, and such as are numerous and apt to fall gracefully into their cadences and periods, and so recommend themselves at the very first sight, as it were; others, which (like false stones) will never shine, in whatever light they be placed, but embase the rest. And here I note that such as have lived long in Universities doe greatly affect words and expressions no where in use

> besides, as may be observed in Cleavelands' Poems for
> Cambridg; and there are also some Oxford words us'd
> by others, as I might instance in severall.[12]

This comes under the heading of 'exotic words'. As far as
Evelyn was concerned, Cleveland's poems were written 'for
Cambridg'. The difference, in fact, between Donne's language and Cleveland's is that between an educated man
talking intelligently to his equals and a specialist talking
shop.

Since the whole point of Cleveland's technical language,
and, indeed, of his poems themselves, was to show off the
writer's ingenuity and resources, Cleveland and his followers never really managed to say anything for themselves. They were too busy straining after cleverness and
nudging their readers into the appreciation of their esoteric
jokes. This is why none of them, despite their moments of
inflation, ever wrote a serious poem. (The one exception
is Cleveland's powerful 'Epitaph on the Earl of Strafford';
and that may not be by him.) All criteria fell before the
need to be clever, both what the Elizabethans called 'decorum'—the formal matching of style to occasion—and that
more flexible but basically similar standard which came
out of Donne's personal realism, and is known simply as
tact. This, for example, from Cleveland's famous poem on
Edward King, the subject of 'Lycidas':

> I am no poet here; my pen's the spout
> Where the rain-water of mine eyes runs out
> In pity of that name, whose fate we see
> Thus copied out in grief's hydrography.
> The Muses are not mermaids, though upon
> His death the ocean might turn Helicon.

Perhaps there is supposed to be a parallel between the ex-
cessiveness of his grief and the galvanic leaps and bounds
of his wit. But even if there were, the concept of wit has
clearly altered a good deal since the earlier days of the
School of Donne. Instead of being an individual power by
which the poet discriminates and synthesizes his material,
wit has become a simple mechanism for turning out novel
and learned periphrases.

Cleveland, however, undeniably had a talent for reducing

[12] J. E. Spingarn, *Critical Essays of the Seventeenth Century*,
Oxford, 1908, II, pp. 311-12.

everything into terms of his own monolithic pedantry, even
the theme of Carew's 'Rapture' and of many of Donne's
'Elegies':

> Mystical grammar of amorous glances;
>   Feeling of pulses, the physic of love;
> Rhetorical courtings and musical dances;
>   Numbering of kisses arithmetic prove;
>   Eyes like astronomy;
>   Straight-limbed geometry;
>   In her arts ingeny
>   Our wits were sharp and keen.

He was, all things considered, remarkably single-minded
in his devotion to scholastic discipline.

He seems moreover, to have known mostly what he was
about. When he describes his mistress's hand as

> So soft, 'tis air but once removed;
> Tender as 'twere a jelly gloved.

he is not failing to write a serious conceit, he is simply
trying to be amusing, or 'witty' in the modern sense. 'Fus-
cara', in fact, is one of a number of Cleveland's pieces that
are not at all serious poems which have misfired, but are, instead, merely strings of rather dapper jokes and epigrams.

Poetry for Cleveland and his followers was a game of
wit, whose counters were words and whose rules were the
frame of reference to University learning. The game had
two objects: first, to be amusing; second, to exhibit to their
most startling advantage the ingenuity and learning of the
poet. None of these poets, I suggest, ever properly envied
Donne's eminence as a serious and original poet, but they
were very jealous indeed of his title of 'Monarch of Wit'.
Hence they reconceived wit in terms on which they were
able to compete: those of amusing and learned ingenuity.
By doing so, they automatically denied poetry any serious
function. And this, to the rather pragmatic writers of the
Restoration, was unforgivable. So it was with Cleveland's
poetry that the School of Donne finally degenerated and,
because of his popularity—twenty editions, says Saintsbury,
while Milton's 1645 *Poems* had two—that the School was so
willingly held up as a butt for ridicule.

Chapter Seven

ABRAHAM COWLEY

U P to this point all the poets I have discussed have been amateurs. Some, of course, were more amateur than others; while alive, they were known as poets only to a few intimate friends. Others did have volumes of poetry published during their lives, but more perhaps to enhance their reputations as 'wits' than as poets. And the wit was supposed to write verse as just one token of his many abilities. Even Cleveland, one of the most fashionable but also least impressive of the School, was more intent on showing off his intellectual agility and learning than on being a poet. Cowley, however, was different. He was the only member of the School of Donne who was, in a sense, professional. Not that he lived by poetry; he was first a University don and then, while the court was in exile, a personal servant of Queen Henrietta Maria until, like so many others, he made his private peace with Cromwell; he became a fellow of the Royal Society and wrote 'A Proposition for the Advancement of Experimental Philosophy'. But he finished his life under the patronage of the Earl of St Albans and the Duke of Buckingham, and they presumably were supporting a ditinguished poet, not an amateur botanist.

But whether or not he wrote for a living is beside the point. Cowley was the only professional in the School of Donne because he was the only poet to produce theories to support his practice. They were never formally paraded: his 'Discourse Concerning Style', which Sprat mentioned, was hardly begun before his death. Cowley's theories are confined to his prefaces and to his footnotes. But these show that he knew precisely what he was about and was willing to produce peculiarly deliberate reasons for what, in the other Metaphysical poets, were the accidents of the intelligent, intimate style. Dr Johnson remarked that "Cowley's critical abilities have not been sufficiently observed: the few decisions and remarks which his prefaces and his notes on the *Davideis* supply were at that time accessions to English literature, and shew such skill as raises our wish for more examples".[1] Without impugning the impersonal justice of the Doctor's judgment, I suggest he was particularly impressed because Cowley's critical shrewdness operated in an area congenial to, perhaps essentially the same as, that of the rest of the Augustans—Johnson included. He justified his verse by the precedent of the classics and wrote with an awareness of fashionable Continental theorizing. These were the bases of Restoration criticism and the norms for the next hundred-odd years, just as, in a cruder and more haphazardly understood way, they had been behind Renaissance theory. This, I think, is what made for Cowley's extraordinary popularity: he was the first obviously decorous, theoretically justifiable or even recognizable poet in the School of Donne. That is why Sprat, in his life of Cowley, could make him a perfect example of that Restoration ideal, the Man of Sense. (Had the taste gone the other way it would, after all, have been perfectly easy to justify even the extreme Metaphysical style by classical precedent and Continental theory. Donne's contemporaries called him 'Persius' for his satires; Drummond thought he was 'Anacreontick'. There were, moreover, a host of Continental theorists who produced a kind of cosmology of wit which amply justified Marino, and could have as easily done so for Crashaw, even, perhaps, for Cleveland.[2] But these were theories for a special taste, chiefly the Baroque. The main line of theoretical development followed, instead, the *grands maîtres* of classical literature.)

Cowley has one important quality in common with Milton: not the accident of being also an infant prodigy (*Poeticall Blossomes* was published in 1633, when he was 15), but the way in which he set out to earn himself the title of 'great poet' by going deliberately through the required kinds of poetry as established by the classics—that is, by Virgil. I mention this not to show by how much he failed but to suggest how radically different his conception of poetry was from Donne's. Carew, in his elegy on Donne, insisted above everything else on the originality of the man; he did what

[1] Samuel Johnson, 'Cowley', *The Lives of the English Poets*, ed. G. Birkbeck Hill, 2 vols., Oxford, 1905, I, p. 38.

[2] See three articles by J. A. Mazzeo, 'A Critique of Some Modern Theories of Metaphysical Poetry', *Modern Philology*, l., 1952, pp. 88-96; 'A Seventeenth Century Theory of Metaphysical Poetry', *The Romanic Review*, xlii, 1951, pp. 245-55; 'Metaphysical Poetry and the Poetry of Correspondence', *Journal of the History of Ideas*, xiv, 1953, pp. 221-34.

he did by his own powers, without borrowing or even referring to the classics:

> Thou didst pay
> The debts of our penurious bankrupt age;
> Licentious thefts, that make poëtique rage
> A Mimique fury, when our soules must bee
> Possest, or with Anacreons Extasie,
> Or Pindars, not their owne . . .
>   . . . As in time
> They had the start, so did they cull the prime
> Buds of invention many a hundred yeare,
> And lcft the rifled fields, besides the feare
> To touch their Harvest, yet from those bare lands
> Of what is purely thine, thy only hands
> (And that thy smallest worke) have gleaned more
> Than all those times, and tongues could reape before.

Cowley is the exact opposite of this. He was not a plagiarist, but he never wrote a word without the precedent of some other poet. His models were not necessarily Latin or Greek. All that mattered was that they were established. For example, he wrote that extraordinarily dull collection of love poems, *The Mistress* because, he said,

> *Poets* are scarce thought *Free-men* of their *Company,* without paying some duties, and obliging themselves to be true to *Love.* Sooner or later they must all pass through that *Tryal,* like some *Mahumetan Monks,* that are bound by their Order, once at least, in their life, to make a *Pilgrimage to Meca.*[3]

So he adopted the manner, occasions and technique of the acknowledged master of love poetry, Donne, and dutifully wrote a volume of love verses. Johnson was right about the result: "Cowley's *Mistress* has no powers of seduction. . . . His poetical account of the virtues of plants and colours of flowers is not perused with more sluggish frigidity. The compositions are such as might have been written for penance by a hermit, or for hire by a philosophical rhymer who

---

[3] Abraham Cowley, *Poems,* ed. A. R. Waller, Cambridge, 1905, p. 10.

had only heard of another sex," [4] But the curious thing is
that *The Mistress* may have been admired for exactly the
qualities Johnson attacked. The poems may have been frigid,
but they were eminently correct. And this deepens Johnson's
remarks about the shrewdness of Cowley's criticism: a good
deal of his *poetry* is fundamentally critical; it is based on
his ability to analyse some other poet's work and then repro-
duce the techniques, suitably chastened and corrected according to his own and the time's lights. He admitted that
this was the method he used in translating Pindar. He did the
same when he translated Donne into Restoration terms.

He even managed to find classical precedent for the most
denigrated elements of the strong line: its harshness and
far-fetched conceits. That, he claimed, was the way Pindar
wrote:

> The *Figures* are unusual and *bold*, even to *Temeritie*,
> and such as I durst not have to do withal in any other
> kind of *Poetry:* The *Numbers* are various and irregu-
> lar, and sometimes (especially some of the long ones)
> seem harsh and uncouth, if the just measures and ca-
> dencies are not observed in the *Pronunciation*. So that
> almost all their *Sweetness* and *Numerosity* (which is to
> be found, if I mistake not, in the roughest, if rightly
> repeated) lies in a manner wholly at the *Mercy* of the
> *Reader*.[5]

Hence you find Sprat declaring:

> If any are displeas'd at the boldness of his Metaphors
> and length of his Digressions they contend not against
> Mr *Cowley,* but *Pindar* himself, who was so much rev-
> erenc'd by all Antiquity that the place of his Birth was
> preserv'd as Sacred.[6]

In passing, it seems that, though Metaphysical poetry as
we now know it had substantially disappeared by 1670,[7] it had
a kind of crude cousin which survived well into the Augustan age: the Pindaric Ode. In this the qualities of the strong

[4] *Loc. cit.*, p. 42.

[5] *Loc. cit.*, p. 11.

[6] Thomas Sprat, *An Account of the Life and Writings of Mr
Abraham Cowley*, 1668, Spingarn, II, pp. 131-2.

[7] The last seventeenth-century edition of Donne's poems was in
1669.

line, harshness and extreme, obscure, learned metaphors were dispersed in lengthy, digressive rhetoric and sanctified in the name of a Greek poet. Pindarics were, fundamentally, the strong line hallowed and corrected.

The business of finding models and precedent seems to have been something of a programme with Cowley. At times he defends his lapses from regularity by aggressively taking his readers' education in hand:

> I am sorry that it is necessary to admonish the most part of *Readers*, that it is not by *negligence* that this verse is so loose, long, and as it were, *Vast;* it is to paint in the number the nature of the thing which it describes, which I would have observed in divers other places of this *Poem,* that else will pass for very careless verses. . . . This thing is, that the disposition of words and numbers should be such as out of the order and sound of them, the things themselves may be represented. This the *Greeks* were not so accurate as to bind themselves to; neither have our *English Poets* observed it, for ought I can find. The *Latins* . . . sometimes did it, and their *Prince, Virgil,* always.[8]

No doubt this was special pleading. Dr Johnson commented coolly on his examples: "What there is peculiar in the sound of the line expressing *loose care* I cannot discover; nor why the *pine* is *taller* in an Alexandrine than in ten syllables".[9] But the point is simply that irregularity became regular provided a precedent could be found for it. In fact, Cowley was essentially so far from the School of Donne that he was one of the chief helpers in reinstating classical verse as the norm, the point of reference, for English poetry. He bears this out touchingly in a footnote to his epic, the *Davideis:* "For this liberty of inserting an *Ode* into an *Heroick Poem,* I have no authority or example; and therefore like men who venture upon a new coast, I must run the hazard of it. We must sometimes be bold to innovate."[10] And then he quotes Horace to support him in his boldness.

Cowley's importance, however, as the transition poet between the Metaphysicals and the Augustans depends on something more than his frame of reference. After all, Ben Jonson and his tribe were soaked in classical poetry; so was Mar-

8 Waller, p. 273.

9 *Loc. cit.,* p. 62.

10 Waller, p. 277.

vell, so was Milton and so was Waller. Cowley's poetry was a turning-point because it seemed to be following Donne's style, whilst in fact being intensely and fashionably of the Restoration. So there is, in his poetry, a dichotomy not exactly between styles, but between the detail and the general effect. Sprat admitted as much in the process of praising Cowley for his scope and depth:

> We have many things that he writ in two very unlike conditions, in the University and the Court. But in his Poetry as well as his Life, he mingled with excellent skill what was good in both states. In his life he join'd the innocence and sincerity of the Scholar with the humanity and good behaviour of the Courtier. In his Poems he united the Solidity and Art of the one with the Gentility and Gracefulness of the other.[11]

Since Sprat is so obviously making the best of Cowley, this might be expressed in another way: largely because of Cleveland's efforts, the Universities meant a poetry of strong lines, of learning, obscurity, ingenuity and harshness; the Court meant smoothness, a certain polite formality and probably some easy classicizing.[12] Cowley's achievement was to juxtapose these *mores* without essentially changing either of them. The 'Ode of Wit', for example:

> In a true piece of *Wit* all things must be,
>   Yet all things there *agree*.
> As in the *Ark*, joyn'd without force or strife,
> All *Creatures* dwelt; all *Creatures* that had *Life*.
>   Or as the *Primitive Forms* of all
>   (If we compare great things with small)
> Which without *Discord* or *Confusion* lie,
> In that strange *Mirror* of the *Deitie*.

What Cowley has to say has no organic relationship with the illustrations he uses. He even keeps them apart: he says his say first in polite, simple language; then he gives his examples, both from reputable sources (the Bible and Aristotle); for good measure, he throws in a Latinism ("If we

[11] Spingarn, II, p. 128.

[12] F. W. Bateson has pointed out to me that the dominant influence in this was probably the French queen; see Richard Flecknoe's *Miscellanies*, 1653, p. 77: 'In the late Kings dayes the *Queen* having a mayne *ascendancy* and *predominance* in the Court the *French style* with the Courtyers was chiefly in *vogue* and Fashion.'

compare great things with small"). The similes, of course, are efficient, lucid and, relatively, learned. But they are not conceits. For Metaphysical conceits, from Donne's to Cleveland's, are always means of continuing the poet's argument in terms of something else; they are all argued and to a point. And behind their arguments is a further argument: "These things which we discuss in our cooler, more intellectual moments behave in this way, with these results; therefore what I argue about us or myself must be true". The Metaphysical conceit, in short, is an integral part of the argument in a kind of poetry in which the argument is everything.

None of Cowley's imagery has this kind of central logical inevitability nor complexity of reference. (I am speaking now of his most typical and original work, the *Odes, Miscellanies* and *Verses on Several Occasions,* not of his *Mistress,* where he was deliberately aping Donne.) Cowley's method, even his effort, is simpler. Since there is always a gap between what he says and the illustrations he uses, each poem becomes, as it were, two sided; the sides support, illustrate and above all, *simplify* each other.

Cowley's, in fact, is a discursive style, a poetry of discussion not argument. Unlike the rest of the School's verse, it is not particularly difficult; it does not challenge the reader's wit and learning. Where it does, Cowley is always careful to add detailed footnotes to explain what he is doing. It is in one of these footnotes that he sets forth the principles of his imagery. The poem is his Pindaric setting of 'The 34th Chapter of the Prophet *Isaiah*':

> The manner of the *Prophets* writing, especially of *Isaiah,* seems to me very like that of *Pindar;* they pass from one thing to another with almost *Invisible connexions,* and are full of words and expressions of the highest and boldest flights of *Poetry,* as may be seen in this Chapter, where there are as extraordinary Figures as can be found in any *Poet* whatsoever; and the connexion is so difficult, that I am forced to adde a little, and leave out a great deal to make it seem *Sense* to us, who are not used to that elevated way of expression . . . in the Text there be no Transition from the *subject* to the *similitude;* for the old fashion of writing, was like *Disputing* in *Enthymemes,* where half is left out to be supplied by the Hearer: ours is like *Syllogisms,* where all that is meant is exprest.[13]

13 Waller, p. 214.

There is an extraordinary distance between Donne's "I will have no such readers as I can teach" and Cowley's bland assumption that every detail of a poem must be self-explanatory. And Cowley's practice of keeping argument and illustration apart, joining them only by a kind of principle of mutual lucidity is the practical form of a Restoration critical truism: that Judgment and Fancy are the two equal but separate sides of the poetic process. "Judgment", said Hobbes, "begets the strength and structure, and Fancy begets the ornaments of a Poem." [14]

I think this may be what Mr Eliot was referring to when he spoke of "the dissociation of sensibility". But it is not a strange chemical deterioration of the poet's inner processes; the craftsmanly sensibilities of Sidney or Spenser seem to me no more or less unified than those of Milton or Dryden, though they may be less acute. The dissociation came when the poets and critics insisted at all times on clarity: clarity in practice, which meant an essentially simple relationship between what is said and how it is illustrated; and clarity in theory, which meant the simple mechanics of opposing forces —Fancy and Judgment, University and Court, Argument and Ornament, Sense and Simile, and so on.

Naturally, this affected the language and texture of poetry. Cowley, for example, went through the motions of disregarding smooth metres, and Sprat, in his defence, invoked the usual distinction between Masculine and Feminine styles. Yet, despite the occasional roughness, Cowley never managed that air of easy intimate conversation of the other Metaphysicals. There is a veil over his language. This is Cowley addressing his Muse:

> Well: but in Love, thou dost pretend to Reign,
>   There thine the power and Lordship is,
> Thou bad'st me write, and write, and write again;
>   'Twas such a way as could not miss.
>   I like a Fool, did thee Obey,
> I wrote, and wrote, but still I wrote in vain,
> For after all my expense of Wit and Pain,
> A rich, unwriting Hand, carry'd the Prize away.

Compare this with Herbert:

> Whereas my birth and spirit rather took
>   The way that takes the town;

[14] 'Answer to Davenant's Preface to *Gondibert*', 1650, Spingarn, II, p. 59.

> Thou did'st betray me to a lingring book,
>   And wrap me in a gown.
> I was entangled in the world of strife,
> Before I had the power to change my life.

My quotation shows Cowley at his easiest and most colloquial. Yet even his ease seems like a formal device. He is, for instance, extraordinarily repetitive. He makes his points by saying everything two or three times over.

> . . . thou dost pretend to Reign,
> There thine the power and Lordship is.

Herbert, on the other hand, is vivid, because of a kind of physical concentration in his language:

> Thou did'st *betray* me to a *lingring* book,
>   And *wrap* me in a gown.
> I was *entangled.* . . .

The lines are emphatic because they are actual. This, in turn, points to another quality of Cowley's verse: its abstraction. Herbert's poetry is continually referring—through its kind of language and images and its speaking rhythm—to the world of common experience; Cowley's at every point touches a framework of fixed abstractions. He seems continually on the point of reducing his poetry to a general statement. Behind everything, I think, is the concept of Politeness. When, for example, Cowley wants emphasis, he uses formal rhetorical means ("I wrote, and wrote, but still I wrote in vain"), just as, when he wants to praise something, he uses formal, acknowledged abstractions (Wit, Civility, Arts, Trade, and so on). He writes always within the framework of what the Restoration would have called 'acknowledged Truths'. Sprat said of his language:

> in the choice and elegance of his words . . . he had no manner of affectation . . . he took them as he found them made to his hands; he neither went before nor came after the use of the Age. He forsook the Conversation, but never the Language, of the City and Court.[15]

There was, I think, something slightly abstracted about this

[15] *Loc. cit.*, p. 129.

language, as though it implied a formula for politeness. In Chapter 3 I tried to show how Herbert's 'Love (III)' drew part of its strength from a code of manners. But that only made the writing more personal, more delicate, more tactful and, incidentally, more colloquial. Cowley's politeness, however, goes hand in hand with formal rhetoric. It is a more public, more deliberately adhered to, formal process. It implies a recognized norm for polite speech and behaviour, just as behind his metres loom a recognized norm for the polite behaviour of verses. I am not suggesting that Cowley used a specialized language of poetry; he had far too much respect for the world of practical affairs. But he was less concerned with his individual voice than with a recognized and generally acceptable public voice. His politeness in verse was, too, a public manner rather than an instinctive delicacy.

Finally, then, there is the rhythm: Herbert's rather elaborate metrical form runs exactly with natural emphasis of the speaking voice. But Cowley's lines are longer or shorter than the ten-syllable norm, not because his material demands a rapid interplay of rhythms, but simply to avoid *appearing* regular. Is this doctored version any less emphatic than Cowley's original lines?

> Well: but in Love, thou dost pretend to Reign,
> There thine the power, *the life* and Lordship is,
> Thou bad'st me write, and write, and write again;
> 'Twas such a way, *in truth*, as could not miss.
> I like a *triple* Fool, did thee Obey,
> I wrote, and wrote, but still I wrote in vain,
> For after all my expense of Wit and Pain,
> A rich, unwriting Hand, *bore all* away.

I admit I have weakened the image in the last line. Otherwise the lines seem to have lost nothing by their regularity. I suggest, then, that Cowley's irregular metres are not strictly necessary. They serve most to remind you of the norm from which they depart. After all, the only line in which Cowley is irremediably harsh is, in fact, ten-syllabled:

> For after all my expense of Wit and Pain.

The roughness does not make the line particularly personal or emphatic; it merely makes it prose.

In a curious way, this is one of the most important things about Cowley's poetry. Sprat, at least, thought so:

That for which I think this inequality of number is chiefly to be preferr'd is its near affinity with Prose . . . the practice of it will only exalt, not corrupt our Prose, which is certainly the most useful kind of writing of all others, for it is the style of all business and conversation.[16]

This reads now as the most back-handed compliment any poet ever received from an admirer; but it accounts for Cowley's enormous popularity among his contemporaries. They admired him because he was, above everything else, sensible: neither too clever, nor too vague, nor too fantastic, nor too individual, nor too obscure. He was pre-eminently a Man of Sense, reasonable, moderate, polite. And his poetry, precisely when he was innovating most, came nearest to prose, the medium of common sense. By a kind of cheerful reasonableness, he vindicated poetry in an age which distrusted any excess.

Sprat wrote one other document of considerable importance: *The History of the Royal Society of London*. In that he set forth the pragmatic and sensible ideals of his time. His *Account of the Life and Writings of Mr Abraham Cowley*, which appeared the following year (1668) is, as it were, a sequel to the *History*. The Royal Society formulated the ideals; Cowley embodied them. Sprat makes him appear as the archetypal Man of Sense and Judgment, and his discursive, mild, polite poetry as the natural product of these tastes, excellent precisely to the degree to which it abandoned the differences and pretences of poetry. "He had", Sprat said, "a firmness and strength of mind that was of proof against the Art of Poetry it self." [17] It was this kind of formulation and this kind of taste, not, I suspect, their poetry, which made Matthew Arnold brand the great Augustans, Dryden and Pope, 'masters of our prose'.

[16] *Loc. cit.*, p. 132.
[17] *Loc. cit.*, p. 139.

Chapter Eight

THE METAPHYSICALS AND THE METAPHYSICIANS

Nullius in Verba.—Motto of the Royal Society

I

AT the beginning I suggested that one of the odd things about the School of Donne was that the Restoration critics managed to dismiss it finally without any specific criticism. They had none of the usual indignant antagonism of one literary generation shuffling from its back the unbearable weight of another. Nor did they quite have that knowing and effortless superiority of those who have come through; that was left to the later Augustans, settled in their ways; to the essays of the ageing Dryden, to Addison discoursing on Wit, to Pope of *An Essay on Criticism*. The critics during and immediately after the Civil War shied away from the School of Donne as though no discussion of it were even possible. Instead of a fighting criticism, there is only an instinctive withdrawal, as there might have been from, say, Marxist literature during the exertions of the late Senator McCarthy. The Restoration writers found the Metaphysicals faintly suspect, and their reasons were not wholly literary. They objected more to certain things the poets stood for than to their writing.

This was made easier because of that peculiar brand of tough colloquial realism which Donne perfected, the realism that was also the voice of the highly intelligent professional class. This type of poetry was recognizable more precisely as wit—as a way of talking, a social manner—than as a specifically literary procedure.

This, I think, was what was meant when the words 'metaphysics' and 'metaphysical' were used of Donne and his followers. The critics were objecting to a way of talking and a way of thinking, not to a formal theory of poetry. For the words were used long before Dr Johnson named the school or even before Dryden accused Donne of affecting the metaphysics.[1] And they were used always in the same way. The first English appearance of the terms in connection with poetry stands as a cipher for all the rest:

> In vain have some Men of late (Transformers of every Thing) consulted upon her [poetry's] Reformation, and endeavoured to abstract her to *Metaphysical* ideas, and *Scholastical* Quiddities, denuding her of her own Habits, and those Ornaments with which she hath amused the whole World some Thousand Years.[2]

That is from a letter by William Drummond of Hawthornden to Arthur Johnson, probably written between 1625 and 1630. Grudgingly, it makes the usual points about Donne's style: his originality (Drummond finds it misplaced) and his rejection of conventional poetic ornaments. But most important, Drummond is not using 'Metaphysical' as a term of literary criticism. On the contrary, he is using it to imply a lack of literary criteria. It is a synonym of 'scholastical'—that is, associated with the Schoolmen philosophers, the followers of Aquinas and Aristotle. In this Drummond is typical of every critic and poet—Dryden and Pope among them—who used the word, at least until Dr Johnson transformed it into a literary title. Their objection was to an intellectual not a poetic style. It was a style that was becoming unfashionable and, even in Donne's own time, was beginning to be replaced by more empirical scientific methods.

Donne was a powerful, enormously agile and clever master of dialectic; but he was never an advanced thinker in the manner of, say, Bacon. That was not his business. On the contrary, part of his power came from the vitality with which he responded to and used the intellectual training he had been put through. And, like Marlowe's, Jonson's, even Milton's, it was an essentially traditional training. This, I presume, is what Miss Ramsay meant when she called him a mediaeval thinker. He relied heavily on a kind of dialectic that was perfectly in the tradition of the Schoolmen; he was full of references to their two great authorities, Aristotle and Aquinas, and full, too, of sometimes outdated sciences and

---

[1] See A. H. Nethercot, 'The Term "Metaphysical Poet" Before Johnson', *Modern Language Notes*, xxxvii, 1922, p. 11-17; and R. L. Sharp, 'The pejorative uses of *Metaphysical*', *Modern Language Notes*, xlix, 1934, pp. 503-5.

[2] *Familiar Epistles*, No. 14; *The Works of Drummond of Hawthornden*, Edinburgh, 1711, p. 143.

lore, like alchemy and angelology and doctrines of spirits and souls. He was, of course, as perfectly in touch with what was happening in the sciences as with theology; 'new discoveries' of one kind or another turn up frequently. But I think his interest in them was controlled by his rigid intellectual training; that is, he was far more alert to the dialectical sciences, or to sciences amenable to dialectic, than to the experiments and empirical conclusions which were to become the new scientific mode. In these matters, he was essentially traditional. For example, his famous lament that the 'new Philosophy calls all in doubt' has an irony to it that implies at least some sympathy with the old cosmology of the Fathers; and he draws conclusions from the new science to its effects on the hierarchy of society that are wholly traditional. They are much the same as those in the old homily on Obedience, an official sermon, supplied by the State and preached from most of the pulpits in England since the time of Henry VIII. It is, incidentally, much the same sermon on degree as Ulysses preached in *Troilus and Cressida*. So Donne may have been brilliant and original in a way that was new to poetry; but the dialectical form his brilliance took was very much in the intellectual traditions of the time.

Moreover, Donne's reputation itself as a wit was, in one sense, traditional. It was based on his masculine understanding, his command of complex, abstruse arguments and learning and on that intellectual independence which made him remould the style of poetry to suit his own individual intelligence. In fact his wit, as all his elegists said, was a matter of extraordinary personal brilliance. And this in itself became a mark against him. Just as 'cleverness' now is a little suspect, implying a kind of sleight of mind which outwits the reader more than it convinces him, so then dialectical wit began to be rejected in favour of an anonymous but steady experimental procedure. Wit in itself, unaided and independent, was falling rather from fashion and being replaced by 'common sense'.

Finally, Donne's own wit had made way for the deliberately obscure, degenerate wit of the writers of later strong lines, who were difficult and learned merely to disguise the fact that they had so little to say for themselves. Consequently, the Restoration critics viewed Donne from a very low eminence, and with the irrefutable hindsight of those who have seen the *reductio ad absurdum* of a style.

After all, Sprat praised Cowley because:

His Wit was so temper'd that no man had ever reason to wish it had been less: he prevented other mens severity upon it by his own: he never willingly recited any of his Writings. None but his intimate friends ever discovered he was a great Poet by his discourse.[3]

By the Restoration, wit and poetry had become an intrusion against common sense. Instead of showing the temper of the man's mind, it was something itself to be tempered by his practical intelligence. It was an indulgence, a luxury in a climate which was still, in these matters, puritan.

I want to suggest, then, that a 'dissociation of sensibility' —or whatever less loaded term is preferred—*did* take place. But it was not a mysterious chemical deterioration of the minds of the creative writers. Instead, it was general and was based on a deliberate rejection of one kind of intellectual discipline—one way of thinking, in the strictest sense—and the deliberate adoption of another. And for specific reasons. If one ignores the human subtlety and fullness of Donne's work, it is easy, even at this late date, to see him as a kind of poetic Schoolman, instilling into verse the same intellectualism and slightly perverse logical vitality as the Schoolmen had instilled into philosophy. There was, therefore, so little direct contemporary criticism of the School of Donne simply because the critics were able to apply the words 'metaphysical' and 'metaphysics'. This meant they were attributing to him vices that everyone already knew perfectly well and rejected elsewhere.

This does not explain the almost superstitious fear of Metaphysical wit which, I suggested, was the reason for the utter silence on the School of Donne. To do this I want to show first how the non-literary criteria for wit changed, as it were, theoretically; then, how these theories were given force and power by the Civil War, so that this change in the way of thinking was a deliberate, willed adoption of one intellectual style rather than another. Fundamentally, what follows is a background of ideas for Dr Johnson's comments on the Metaphysicals. He was, I suggest, merely expressing in literary terms ideas that had long been accepted in another guise.

II

When Sprat wrote his *Account of the Life and Writings of Mr Abraham Cowley* in 1668 he was doing more than merely writing a personal tribute to a friend. He was also using the life of a distinguished man as a practical example

[3] Sprat, *Life of Cowley*, Spingarn, II, p. 140.

of the ideals he had set forth the year before in his *History of the Royal Society*. The *History* is the theory, the *Life* the practice, of that almost Platonic creation, the Restoration Man of Sense. Behind both stands Bacon: "there should have been", Sprat said "no other Preface to the *History* of the *Royal Society*, but some of his Writings".[4] There also might have been no other epitaph on the School of Donne—though perhaps that is merely saying the same thing in another way.

Yet almost nothing Bacon had to say which became important to literary criticism is to be found in his comments on poetry. He dealt with the subject, of course, but only because the encyclopaedic nature of his great work demanded it: [5] poetry was traditionally one of the three divisions of learning—the others were philosophy and history—which, according to the old faculty psychology, corresponded to the three cells of the brain: imagination foremost, reason in the middle and, at the back of the head, memory. Since Bacon was intent, among other things, on replacing the older Encyclopaedists, he was obliged to refute them on all their grounds. He commented on poetry because comment was traditionally expected; and he commented in a traditional and uninteresting way.

Bacon added only one thing to his conventional discussion of poetry; a fixed distaste for the art. He did not so much discuss it as dispose of it:

> For (poesy) being as a plant that cometh of the lust of the earth, without a formal seed, it hath sprung up and spread abroad more than any other kind. But to ascribe unto it that which is its due; for the expressing of affections, passions, corruptions, and customs, we are beholding to poets' more than to philosophers' works; and for wit and eloquence not much less than to orators' harangues. But it is not good to stay too long in the theatre. Let us now pass to the judicial place or palace of the mind, which we are to approach and view with more reverence and attention.[6]

I suggested at the start that Bacon shared this impatience of

[4] Thomas Sprat, *The History of the Royal Society of London*, 1667, Part I, sec. xvi, p. 35.

[5] See Murray W. Bundy, 'Bacon's True Opinion of Poetry', *Studies in Philology*, xxvii, 1930, pp. 244-64.

[6] *Advancement of Learning*, 2nd Book; *Works of Sir Francis Bacon*, ed. James Spedding, R. Ellis and D. D. Heath, 7 vols., London, 1857-59, III, p. 346.

'whining poetry' with Donne. They both reacted against the pretensions of verse and rhetoric in the name of common sense and rational standards. For this reason they were both exponents of the 'Attic' style. The difference between them is a matter of the kind of reason they adhered to. Donne was largely traditional, and worked within the pattern of his dialectical training. Bacon, on the other hand, was writing a *Great Instauration* in which he put forward a new system of science and reasoning In themselves, his dismissal of poetry and his distrust of the imagination as anything except an auxiliary 'messenger' transmitting sense impressions to the reason and rational commands to the body [7] are not important for my purposes; neither are the details of his new scientific methods. What matters is the way he revalued the importance and duties of the individual reason when faced with the multitudinous, impersonal processes of nature. It amounted to a new view of the importance and function of the intellectual.

The crux of his argument comes at the point where he is discussing his reason for *not* considering poetry seriously:

Poesy, in the sense in which I have defined the word, is also (like History) *concerned with individuals;* that is with individuals invented in imitation of those which are the subject of true history; yet with this difference, that it commonly exceeds the measure of nature, joining *at pleasure* things which in nature would never have come together, and introducing things which in nature would never have come to pass. . . . This is the work of the Imagination.

Philosophy discards individuals; neither does it deal with the impressions immediately received from them, but with the abstract notions derived from these impressions; in the composition and division whereof according to the laws of nature and fact its business lies. And this is the office and work of Reason.[8]

Philosophy discards individuals; that is the essence of

---

[7] See *De Augmentis V,* in *Works,* IV, p. 405. For a full exposition of Bacon's theory of the imagination see Karl R. Wallace, *Francis Bacon on Communication and Rhetoric,* Chapel Hill, 1943. Also Murray W. Bundy, *loc. cit.,* and ' "Invention" and "Imagination" in the Renaissance', *Journal of English and Germanic Philology,* xxix, 1930, pp. 535-45.

[8] *De Augmentis,* II, i; *Works,* IV, p. 292. My italics.

Bacon's intellectual revolution and of whatever it was that the Restoration found so irresistible in his method. The proper subject of poetry is the blight of philosophy: the wilfulness, perhaps, and the conceit, but also the primacy of the individual to judge, analyse and re-create his own experience. Bacon's force and originality was devoted to replacing fallible, self-centred ratiocination with the difficult impersonality of natural experiment and observation:

> All depends on keeping the eye steadily fixed upon the facts of nature and so receiving their images simply as they are. For God forbid we should give out a dream of our own imagination for a pattern of the world.[9]

Imagination here is not, by Bacon's lights, virtuous. It is not the disciplined messenger between sense, reason and action. It is ingenuity; the mind working, building upon itself, or holding, at best, a warping, magnifying mirror before the entranced reason. It sounds much like his remark that "poesy is as a dream of learning".[10] Yet his subject is not the imagination of the poets; it is, instead, the intellect of the Schoolmen. But his objections and his method of attack are fundamentally the same:

> Another error hath proceeded from too great a reverence, and a kind of adoration of the mind and understanding of man; by means whereof men hath withdrawn themselves too much from the contemplation of nature and the observations of experience, and have tumbled up and down in their own reason and conceits. . . . These intellectualists . . . are not-withstanding commonly taken for the most sublime and divine philosophers . . . for they disdain to spell and so by degrees read in the volume of God's works; and contrariwise by continual meditation and agitation of wit do urge and as it were invocate their own spirits to divine and give oracles unto them, whereby they are deservedly deluded.[11]

Bacon charged the Schoolmen with precisely that disregard of fact and reliance on strength of wit which he had found running unchecked in poetry; for quarrying, that is, in 'the depths of the mind', instead of in nature; for creating a feigned philosophy, as poetry was a 'feigned history'; for

---

[9] *The Great Instauration*. 'Plan of the Work'; *Works*, IV, pp. 32-3.
[10] *De Augmentis*, III, i; *Works*, IV, p. 336.
[11] *The Advancement of Learning*, First Book; *Works*, III, p. 292.

relying, in short, on reason driven by imagination, which is how I would define Donne's wit. The materials, of course, differed. Poetry was the imagination playing, with more or less control, variations on the passions and actions of individuals. Scholastic logic played with reason, with arguments and words, and exalted them; or rather, the individual was exalted by the skill with which he exercised his powers of abstract reasoning, by his ingenuity with words and logical formulae. The reason of the Schoolmen hovered lopsidedly in the air, as little anchored to fact as the poetic imagination.

Bacon, in fact, never discussed any poetry that could remotely be thought of as like Donne's. From the start he dismissed as worthless all short poems and confined himself to three classes of verse: *Narrative,* "a mere imitation of History, such as might pass for real, only that it commonly exaggerates beyond probability"; *Dramatic,* "History made visible"; and *Parabolical,* "typical History, by which ideas that are of the intellect are represented in forms that are objects of the sense".[12] But he attacked both Poetry and Scholastic logic as abuses of reality one by the imagination, the other by the intellect—so it would not have been hard for his followers to bundle the two together. And he accused the Schoolmen of 'conceits' and 'agitation of wit' which came from the exact procedure Donne's elegists urged: "a reverence and a kind of adoration of the mind and understanding". So Dryden, it appears was being neither perverse nor paradoxical when he announced: "I may safely say of this present age, that if we are not so great wits as Donne, yet certainly we are better poets." [13]

Fundamentally, Bacon's theories depended upon an attitude to language which, in turn, depended on a kind of Puritanism of the imagination. For imagination, wrongly used, inflames "the affections and perturbations which are, as I have said, the diseases of the mind". And imagination itself is worked on by rhetoric. So the first two 'distempers of learning', of which Bacon's new, sane and healthy philosophy had to rid itself, were rhetoric, "when men study words and not matter", and its twin brother, a deliberate verbal obscurity and abstraction of matter, a kind of rhetoric of the intellect:

12 *De Augmentis,* II, xiii; *Works,* IV, p. 315.
13 'Of the Origin and Progress of Satire', 1693. *Essays of John Dryden,* ed. W. P. Ker, Oxford, 1900, 2 vols., II, p. 102.

The second (distemper of learning) . . . is in nature worse than the former; for as substance of matter is better than beauty of words, so contrariwise vain matter is worse than vain words. . . . Surely, like as many substances in nature which are solid do putrefy and corrupt into worms, so it is the property of good and sound knowledge to putrefy and dissolve into a number of subtile, idle, unwholesome, and (as I may term them) vermiculate questions, which have indeed a kind of quickness and life of spirit, but no soundness of matter or goodness of quality. This kind of degenerate learning did chiefly reign amongst the schoolmen; who having sharp and strong wits, and abundance of leisure, and small variety of reading; but their wits being shut up in the cells of a few authors (chiefly Aristotle their dictator) as their persons were shut up in the cells of monasteries and colleges; and knowing little history, either of nature or time; did out of no great quantity of matter and infinite agitation of wit, spin out unto us those laborious webs of learning which are extant in their books. For the wit and mind of man, if it work upon matter, which is the contemplation of the creatures of God, worketh according to the stuff and is limited thereby; but if it work upon itself, as the spider worketh his web, then it is endless, and brings forth indeed cobwebs of learning, admirable for the fineness of thread and work, but of no substance of profit.[14]

I invite the reader to ponder on this less as an attack on the Schoolmen than as a first draft for Dr Johnson's essay on the Metaphysicals: it has the same distinction between men of intellect and men of the world and practical intelligence, the same criticism of their difficult, learned but useless games of wit, and the same grudging and dismissive admiration. Just as Bacon's first distemper of learning could be stretched to include the florid laxities of the 'feminine' style of poetry, so the second distemper could take in the logical and polysyllabic obscurities of the 'masculine, strong lines'.

Bacon proposed two remedies for these distempers. The first was to get rid of equivocations, ambiguities, and hence of the disputations that fed on them, by rigidly defining all terms at the outset of philosophical discussions.[15] The sec-

---

[14] *The Advancement of Learning*, First Books; *Works*, III, p. 285.
[15] See *De Augmentis*, V, iv; *Works*, IV, p. 431; and *The Advancement of Learning*, Second Book; *Works*, III, p. 394.

ond was to change the object of attention: the business of philosophy should no longer be words, formulae and logical procedures, based on the authority of Aristotle; it should be nature herself: "One who philosophizes rightly and in order, should dissect nature and not abstract her".[16] Bacon proposed, in short, to substitute scientific procedures for logical but verbal abstractions. The details of how precisely he intended to do this do not matter. What is important is the complete change of focus: nature instead of the mind, ingenuity, wit and logic-chopping; or, to use the catch-phrase of the Royal Society, no longer words but things.

This turning upside-down of philosophy had, in a strange way, a direct effect on poetry. The reason is that Bacon was at the same time turning upside down the traditional concept of the powers and importance of the mind of man. He deliberately and systematically downgraded wit by comparing it with the infinite subtlety of nature.

The end of this was to suggest a new concept and function of the understanding. The old, witty, logical style was to go; there was to be no more abstraction and sophistry and verbalizing: "The understanding must not therefore be supplied with wings, but rather hung with weights, to keep it from leaping and flying".[17] At the same time, the other kind of understanding, which registers and orders the evidence of the senses, was to be sharpened, made, by proper scientific procedures, more of a match for the complexities of nature:

> But this I say not to disable the intellect, or to urge the abandonment of enterprise; but to stir men to provide the intellect with proper helps for overcoming the difficulties and obscurities of nature. For no steadiness of hand or amount of practice will enable a man to draw a straight line or perfect circle by hand alone, which is easily done by help of a ruler or compass. And this is the very thing which I am preparing and labouring at with all my might,—to make the mind of man by help of art a match for the nature of things; to discover an art of Indication and Direction, whereby all other arts with their axioms and works may be detected and brought to light.[18]

[16] On Principles and Origins; Works, IV, p. 466.
[17] Novum Organum: First Book of Aphorisms, No. civ; Works, IV, p. 97.
[18] De Augmentis, V, ii; Works, IV, p. 412.

In the place of wit and verbalized intellect Bacon substituted predictable and controllable techniques. The essence of his *Great Instauration* was the displacement of the individual by techniques. Talents, intellect, private effort were useless on their own; they became worthwhile only when directed to the community of experiment. Of course, even the Royal Society had to admit that Bacon's experiments were primitive. But his theories became their working principles, and the whole Restoration concept of politeness is, I think, founded on Bacon's most significant conclusion:

> The course I propose for the discovery of sciences is such as leaves but little to the acuteness and strength of wits, but places all wits and understandings nearly on a level.[19]

Restoration decorum is essentially different from that of the Elizabethans largely because it is no longer a literary procedure. Instead of being a matter of varying the style with the subject, it is a fixed principle of behaviour, almost of conformity, a determination to avoid all bad habits, all emphatic gestures that might seem out of place in, to use Sprat's words, 'the City and Court'. It is, in fact, a principle of mediocrity. And Bacon was the first to suggest that this might be a positive good. This is why Dryden, an eminently witty poet, denied that he was as witty as Donne, why Sprat made such a point of Cowley's reticence about his poetry, and why Davenant, who at times rather fancied himself as a wit in the tradition of Donne, parroted at length Bacon's principle of the equality and fraternity of intelligence in his preface to that epic of wit, *Gondibert*.[20]

All this is at the opposite extreme to the 'Monarchy of Wit', to the ease and intellectual autonomy of the Metaphysical poet, whose poems stood in judgment over the Understander, while the latter attempted, more or less desperately, to follow the subtleties of thought, feeling and reference. In place of all this, Bacon proposed a levelling out of the understanding by scientific techniques which made all men equal before nature. The intellect, supplied with the aids of experiment, was no longer to be concerned with itself or with its counters, words. With this denigration of a wit that was individual, abstracting and, in a word, metaphysical, went a dis-

---

[19] *Novum Organum*, First Book of Aphorisms, No. lxi; *Works*, IV, p. 62. See also *idem.*, No. cxxii, p. 109.

[20] See Spingarn, II, pp. 7-8.

trust of all rhetoric and its province—the imagination and the passions—unless meticulously circumscribed. It is an ideal of man as a creature strictly limited, made almost impersonal in the community of science. In short, before 1620 Bacon had sketched out in detail the Man of Sense and the poetic ideals of the Restoration.

There are two obvious objections to this: the first is that Bacon never shows any sign of being aware of Donne's new style; so to apply to literature his criticisms of a philosophical style is merely perverse special pleading. I would counter this by showing that his criticisms of the Schoolmen were directly linked and usually juxtaposed with his attacks on rhetoric, poetry and the falsities of the imagination. It would be perfectly natural for later writers to think of both, however obscurely, as 'the enemy'. The second objection is that philosophical theories, particularly those of natural philosophy or science, usually have, at least, a peculiarly remote effect on poetry and literary criticism. The reply to this is twofold: first, Bacon's theories implied a new concept of the whole importance of the mind, which certainly has a bearing on both poetry and criticism; second, the writers of the middle of the seventeenth century had a single, cogent and compelling reason for adopting these standards of impersonality and factual clarity: namely, the Civil War.

III

Bacon pioneered the ground but it was Hobbes, Bacon's secretary, who consolidated it. He brought the Metaphysicals and the Schoolmen into the focus of a single vice—the abuse of language—which he attacked not just for itself but as a means of sedition.

Hobbes's critiques are both more complex and clearer than Bacon's. The reason is that he was himself a poet and at times a very good critic. Dryden called him "our poet and philosopher of Malmesbury" [21] and compared him to Lucretius, while Anthony à Wood, in a catalogue of his skills and virtues, calls him "a great critic and poet".[22] It hardly matters that his own verse was poor, dull and mostly in Latin. The effort of writing embroiled him in literature. So his interest was not, like Bacon's, a duty; it was alive and contem-

[21] Preface to *Sylvae*, 1685, in *Essays*, ed. W. P. Ker, I, p. 259.

[22] *Atheniae Oxonienses*, ed. Philip Bliss, 1817, III, p. 1208.
Both of these quotations are also to be found in Clarence De Witt Thorpe, *The Aesthetic Theory of Thomas Hobbes*, Ann Arbor, 1940, pp. 3-9, which gives a full picture of Hobbes as a literary man.

porary. There is no difficulty in accommodating what he said about wit and the needs of good verse to describe whatever we now admire in Donne. Moreover his comments are, for my purposes, much sharper than Bacon's because he not only must have known the work of Donne and his earlier followers; he had also seen the corruption of the style into the game of wit and strong lines. So he attacked something quite definite and, for anyone as seriously interested in poetry as Hobbes was, something that very much needed attacking; and he gave his reasons.

Hobbes had something in common with the modern Oxford philosophers: he rested his philosophy squarely on language:

> True and False are attributes of Speech, not of Things. And where Speech is not, there is neither Truth nor Falshood. Errour there may be . . .[23]

Language, in short, was a basic *fact* of society. Therefore, a sane, stable society—the subject of *Leviathan*—must have for its use a clear, stably defined vocabulary. In effect, if not in theory, this meant that he reduced good and bad, right and wrong in almost everything to a question of the clarity or obscurity of language. He followed Bacon's lead in insisting that to save the failing health of philosophy all discourse should begin with rigid definitions which had thereafter to be adhered to.

As with Bacon, I am not concerned with Hobbes's philosophical or political theories except where they touch on poetry. Mercifully, he was a consistent thinker; he tended, in fact, to repeat himself. Consequently there is a direct relationship between his philosophical and literary theories. He uses the same criteria for both disciplines. This, for example, is his definition of good poetic style:

> For the order of words, when placed as they ought to be, carries a light before it, whereby a man may foresee the length of his period, as a torch in the night shews a man the stops and unevenness in his way. But when plac'd unnaturally, the Reader will often find unexpected checks, and be forced to go back and hunt for the sense, and suffer such unease, as in a Coach a man unexpectedly finds in passing over a furrow.[24]

[23] *Leviathan*, I, iv, p. 15.
[24] 'The Vertues of an Heroique Poem', Spingarn, II, p. 69.

It is the same, even to the metaphor, as good philosophy:

> The Light of humane minds is Perspicuous Words, but
> by exact definitions first snuffed, and purged from am-
> biguity; *Reason* is the *pace;* Encrease of *Science,* the
> *way;* and the Benefit of man-kind, the *end.* And on the
> contrary, Metaphors, and senslesse and ambiguous words,
> are like *ignes fatui;* and reasoning upon them, is wander-
> ing amongst innumerable absurdities, and their end,
> contention, and sedition, or contempt.[25]

There is nothing very remarkable about either of these
requirements, except in that last sentence. A clear, unambig-
uous style is not simply desirable in itself, it is a social duty.
Without it, there is chaos.

It is this that gives an edge and an importance to his attack on the abuses of poetry:

> There be so many words in use at this day in the English
> Tongue, that *though of magnifique sound, yet . . . have
> no sense at all,* and so many others that lose their mean-
> ing by being ill coupled, that it is a hard matter to avoid
> them; for having been obtruded upon youth in the
> Schools by such as make it, I think, their business there
> (as 'tis exprest by the best Poet)
>
> *With terms to charm the weak and pose the wise,*
>
> they grow up with them, and, *gaining reputation with
> the ignorant,* are not easily shaken off. To this palpable
> darkness I may also add *the ambitious obscurity of ex-
> pressing more then is perfectly conceived,* or perfect
> conception in fewer words than it requires. Which Ex-
> pressions, though they have had the honor to be called
> strong lines, are indeed no better than Riddles, and, not
> onely to the Reader but also after a little time to the
> Writer himself, dark and troublesome.[26]

These are precisely the charges he made against the Schoolmen:

> There is yet another fault in the Discourses of some
> men; which may also be numbred amongst the sorts of

[25] *Leviathan,* I, v, p. 22.
[26] 'Answer to Davenant', Spingarn, II, p. 63. Mostly my italics.

Madnesse; namely, that *abuse of words,* whereof I have spoken before . . . by the Name of Absurdity. And that is, when men speak *such words as put together, have in them no signification at all;* but are fallen upon by some, through misunderstanding of the words they have received, and repeat by rote; by others, *from intention to deceive by obscurity.* And this is incident to *none but those, that converse in questions of matters incomprehensible, as the Schoolemen;* or in questions of abstruse Philosophy.[27]

The Writings of Schoole-Divines, are nothing else for the most part, but *insignificant Traines of strange and barbarous words,* or words otherwise used, then in the common use of the Latine tongue; . . . Which if any man would see proved, let him . . . see whether he can translate any Schoole-Divine into any of the Modern tongues . . . for that which cannot in most of these be made Intelligible, is not Intelligible in the Latine. Which Insignificancy of language, though I cannot note it for false Philosophy; yet it hath a quality, not onely to hide the Truth, but also to make men think they have it, and desist from further search.[28]

They, too, suffered 'from intention to deceive by obscurity'. But their purpose was not merely to glorify their wit; it was to gain control over the minds of men:

The *Ecclesiastiques* take from young men, the use of Reason, by certain Charms compounded of Metaphysiques, and Miracles, and Traditions, and Abused Scripture, whereby they are good for nothing else, but to execute what they command them.[29]

These are the same ingredients as those of Metaphysical verse, and the degenerate forms of both verse and philosophy had the same aim: that is, the riddle, the charm which works on the vanity of the clever who manage to solve it, and on the supersitition of the ignorant who revere, because they cannot understand, whatever is hard and abstruse. The difference is that where the strong-lined poets were merely pretentious, tiresome and pedantic, the Schoolmen were dangerous. Hobbes

[27] *Leviathan,* I, viii, pp. 39-40. My italics.
[28] *Leviathan,* IV, xlvi, p. 375. My italics.
[29] *Idem,* IV, xlvii, p. 382.

used them as his whipping-boys not just because he disliked their kind of philosophy and the kind of academic conservatism which still supported it,[30] but primarily because they had been, he thought, one of the means by which Rome had maintained its power in England. And his objections to this were less religious—Hobbes was attacked in his own time for having no religious convictions at all—than political. Scholastical divinity—metaphysics—did more than obscure faith. Its method was disputation and obscurantism. It nourished, by that, 'contention, sedition' to split the Commonwealth and inject ignorance and superstition into the whole tissue of society, finally bringing on that most malignant and fearsome disease, Civil War:

> As there have been Doctors, that hold there be three Soules in a man: so there be also that think there may be more Soules, (that is, more Soveraigns,) than one, in a Commonwealth; and set up a *Supremacy* against the *Soveraignty; Canons* against *Lawes;* and a *Ghostly Authority* against the *Civill;* working on mens minds, with words and distinctions, that of themselves signifie nothing, but bewray (by their obscurity) that there walketh (as some think invisibly) another Kingdome, as it were a Kingdome of Fayries, in the dark. Now seeing it is manifest, that the Civill Power, and the Power of the Commonwealth is the same thing; and that Supremacy, and the Power of making Canons, and granting Faculties implyeth a Common-wealth; it followeth, that where one is Soveraign, another Supreme; where one can make Lawes, and another make Canons; there must needs be two Common-wealths, of one & the same Subjects; which is a Kingdome divided in it selfe, and cannot stand. . . . When therefore these two Powers oppose one another, the Commonwealth cannot but be in great danger of Civill warre, and Dissolution. For the *Civill* Authority being more visible, and standing in the cleerer light of naturall reason, cannot choose but draw to it in all times a very considerable part of the people: And the *Spirituall,* though it stand in the darknesse of Schoole distinctions, and hard words; yet because the fear of Darknesse, and Ghosts, is greater

[30] "In his last days, after he had been exasperated by certain academicians, he express'd himself in his writing an enemy to the universities, scholastical divinity, metaphysics, Aristotle, Duns Scotus, etc." Anthony à Wood, *loc. cit.*

than other fears, cannot want a party sufficient to Trouble, and sometimes to Destroy a Common-wealth.[31]

The position was this: Man, understanding clearly, behaved rationally, which meant he preserved himself by preserving a safe and sane society. But the Church of Rome had used deliberate obscurity to cloud the understanding, to trade on ignorance for seditious ends, to foster superstition and finally to split the Common-wealth for the furtherance of its own power. Peace and social stability, then, rested on reason and freedom from obscurity and equivocation. Clarity became a civil duty. Hobbes himself set the example by beginning all his works with a rigid definition of terms.

The Kingdom of Darkness ruled by the darkness of the understanding. And the darkness of the strong line was altogether too similar to be tolerated. From the start, the School of Donne was the centre of a cult of wit or intellect, which earned it a reputation for wilful obscurity: obscurity of logical syntax, of vocabulary, of reference. That was a large part of its charm for those who liked it. Moreover, the references were, time and again, to Aristotle and Aquinas, to speculative metaphysics, scholastic lore and outmoded science. The Metaphysicals, in fact, had had about their work all the inconveniences of scholastic metaphysics. Bacon rejected on scientific and epistemological principle everything on which the school relied. Hobbes specifically criticized its major feature, the obscurity. And he saw that not as a mere unfortunate trick of style but as part of a much wider and more dangerous abuse which, in other circumstances, amounted to a conspiracy against the commonwealth of common sense. His arguments were more specific and more urgent than Bacon's; he knew what decadent Metaphysical poetry was—polysyllabic, punning and trivial—and, far more important, he had seen the Civil War. The thinking that dismissed a style of poetry because it had vices in common with a style of philosophy was, perhaps, like that of a Communist witch-hunt, associational, confused and emotive, founded on fear and defensiveness. Perhaps the whole of the Augustan cult of Reason was no more than inverted superstition. But it was no less congent for that.

IV

I suggested that in Sprat's *History of the Royal Society* were the theories of that Restoration ideal, the Man of Sense.

31 *Leviathan*, II, xxix, pp. 174-5.

They are formed from the strands I have been trying so far to separate: a new object of philosophical attention, things instead of abstractions and words; hence a new attitude to language and to the mode of argument; hence, too, a new concept of the function and limitations of the intellect; and behind all this the fear of war, chaos, instability and obscurity.

There is very little in Sprat's *History* that cannot be found more or less developed in Bacon. Sprat admitted this and no one is likely to gainsay him. The one difference is made by the looming shadow of the Civil War. Nature was not, as it was to Bacon, simply a great and complex field that had been ignored in favour of abstractions. Or rather, it was all that and, at the same time, it was also a relief from what was going on in England at the time. Nature was solid, sure, definite and safely impersonal at the very moment when people felt they were being rolled by uncontrollable and indifferent forces:

> (During the Civil War) To have been eternally musing on *Civil business*, and the distresses of their *Country*, was too melancholy a reflexion: It was *Nature* alone, that could pleasantly entertain them, in that estate. The contemplation of that, draws our minds off from past, or present misfortunes, and makes them conquerors over things, in the greatest publick unhappiness: while the consideration of *Men*, and *humane affairs*, may affect us, with a thousand various disquiets; *that* never separates us into mortal Factions; *that* gives us room to differ, without animosity; and permits us, to raise contrary imaginations upon it, without any danger of a *Civil War*.[32]

Similarly, Sprat insisted on the Royal Society's complete intellectual equality not just to counteract the Schoolmen's tiresome conceit of intellect and their overvaluation of verbal tricks. Behind that democracy of the mind, which was the Royal Society, was a fear of argument as such. For 'hard indigestible *arguments*, or sharp *contentions*'[33] are Civil Wars in miniature. They can raise the same kind of passion and arrogance and vindictiveness:

> Nor have they been onely free from *Faction*, but from

[32] *The History of the Royal Society of London*, 1667, Pt. II, sec. ii, p. 56.

[33] *Idem*, II, xxviii, p. 152.

the very *Causes,* and *beginnings* of it. It was in vain for any man amongst them to strive to preferr himself before another; or to seek for any great glory from the subtilty of his Wit; seeing that it was the inartificial process of the *Experiment,* and not the *Acuteness* of any Commentary upon it, which they have had in veneration. There was no room left, for any to attempt, to heat their own, or others minds, beyond a due temper; where they were not allow'd to expatiate, or amplifie, or correct specious arguments together.[34]

It is that last sentence which matters most: I suggested that Bacon spoke of the evils of rhetoric and of false logic as two separate distempers of learning which had roughly similar effects. But here Sprat is crediting logic and intellectual competition with precisely the same powers as those of rhetoric: they heat '(the) mind, beyond a due temper'. In short, the logical, analytical, verbalizing intellect is distrusted and downgraded in exactly the same manner and for exactly the same reasons as the lying, false 'imaginations of *Poets*', with which, he remarked, "their fellow-creatures . . . have long bin vex'd".[35]

In the place of all this Sprat proposed a new kind of wit and poetry based on observable facts of nature, on common sense and on 'the *Arts* of mens hands'. It was to be wholly at one with his principle of the democracy of the intellect: that is, 'intelligible to all' and using "images that are generally observ'd and . . . familiar to mens minds".[36] To prove that this new Royal Society style of verse was necessary as well as desirable he dismissed, briefly but finally, all the other styles and their sources of imagery. Among these is the Metaphysical:

> The *Sciences* of mens brains are none of the best Materials for this kind of *Wit.* Very few have happily succeeded in *Logical, Metaphysical, Grammatical,* nay even scarce in *Mathematical Comparisons;* and the reason is, because they are most of them conversant about things remov'd from the Senses, and so cannot surprize the *fancy* with very obvious, or quick, or sensible delights.[37]

[34] *Idem*, II, xiv, pp. 91-2.
[35] *Idem*, III, xxxv, p. 416.
[36] *Idem*, III, xxxv, p. 415.
[37] *Idem*, III, xxxv, p. 415. Compare this with John Hoskyns, *Directions for Speech and Style,* ed. Hoyt H. Hudson, Princeton, 1935, p. 39. See p. 142, below.

The wit of the School of Donne, in fact, is exactly the same as that of the Schoolmen: it is 'of mens brains' intellectual and abstract, highly verbalized and dialectical. Because Sprat knew broadly, if not in detail, what the essentials of the new style must be—factual, clear and commonsensical—and because he knew very clearly the dangers of the 'sciences of mens brains', he dismissed this intellectual style of poetry out of hand and with only a token comment. But the adjectives he used—*Logical, Metaphysical, Grammatical*—meant that the incipient identification of the School men and the School of Donne was now complete. So complete, in fact, that Sprat's criticism of the philosophers literally became, with relatively minor changes, the most important and famous criticism of the Metaphysicals:

> . . . The *Schole-men*. Whose works when I consider, it puts into my thoughts, how farre more important a good Method of thinking, and a right course of apprehending things, does contribute towards the attaining of perfection in true knowledge, then the strongest, and most vigorous wit in the World, can do without them. It cannot without injustice be deny'd, that they were men of extraordinary strength of mind: they had great quickness of imagination, and subtilty of distinguishing: they very well understood the consequence of propositions: their natural endowments were excellent: their industry commendable: But they lighted on a wrong path at first, and wanted matter to contrive. . . . In brief, *disputing* is a very good instrument, to sharpen mens wits and to make them versatil, and wary defenders of the Principles, which they already know: but it can never much augment the *solid substance of Science* itself. . . . I hope, it will be granted, that the force and vigour of their Wit did more hurt, then good: and onely serv'd to carry them the faster out of the right way, when they were once going.[38]

Dr Johnson had certainly read Sprat's *Life of Cowley* before he wrote his own; he refers to it. I suggest that he also looked at the *History of the Royal Society,* for he makes precisely the same points as Sprat: about the learning, strength of intellect, quickness of imagination and wrong method of the Metaphysicals:

[38] *Idem*, I, ix, pp. 15, 18-19.

The metaphysical poets were men of learning, and to shew their learning was their whole endeavour; but, unluckily resolving to shew it in rhyme, instead of writing poetry they only wrote verses . . . they neither copied nature nor life; neither painted the forms of matter nor represented the operations of the intellect. Those however who deny them to be poets allow them to be wits. . . . Their thoughts are often new, but seldom natural; they are not obvious, but neither are they just; and the reader, far from wondering that he missed them, wonders more frequently by what perverseness of industry they were ever found . . . their learning instructs, and their subtlety surprises; but the reader commonly thinks his improvement dearly bought, and, though he sometimes admires, is seldom pleased. . . . It is with great propriety that subtlety, which in its original import means exility of particles, is taken in its metaphorical meaning for nicety of distinction. Those writers who lay on the watch for novelty could have little hope of greatness; for great things cannot have escaped former observation. Their attempts were always analytick: they broke every image into fragments, and could no more represent by their slender conceits and laboured particularities the prospects of nature or the scenes of life, than he who dissects a sun-beam with a prism can exhibit the wide effulgence of a summer noon. . . . Yet great labour directed by great abilities is never wholly lost: if they frequently threw away their wit upon false conceits, they likewise sometimes struck out unexpected truth: if their conceits were farfetched, they were often worth the carriage. To write on their plan, it was at least necessary to read and think. . . . If their greatness seldom elevates their acuteness often surprises; if the imagination is not always gratified, at least the powers of reflection and comparison are employed; and in the mass of materials, which ingenious absurdity has thrown together, genuine wit and useful knowledge may be sometimes found, buried perhaps in grossness of expression, but useful to those who know their value . . . the authors of this race were perhaps more desirous of being admired than understood.[39]

[39] Samuel Johnson, *Lives of the English Poets,* ed. George Birkbeck Hill, 2 vols., Oxford, 1905; 'Cowley', I, pp. 19-23.

There are two differences between the passages: first, the Doctor has turned Sprat's charges into specifically literary criticism: 'metaphysical' may still mean 'like the scholastic metaphysicians', but the failings and absurdities are now more strictly literary. Second, unlike Sprat, Johnson asserts that the Metaphysicals never 'represented the operations of the intellect'. This does not, I think, undercut my argument. It simply means that, by the time Dr Johnson wrote, the operations of the intellect *had* changed; the reforms Sprat advocated had come to pass, though in a way neither so drastic nor so simple as he imagined. The world was not suddenly peopled with industrious experimenters, but the intense scientific practicality, common sense and clarity of the Royal Society had been transformed into the Augustans' reasonable sense of fact: into their acute but no less practical awareness of their social duties, their concentration on the facts of the World, which is what they called society, beyond which lay the great, lucid moral generalities.

The heart of the matter is in two sentences of the Doctor's. The first is not quoted above:

> As they were wholly employed on something unexpected and surprising they had no regard to that uniformity of sentiment, which enables us to conceive and to excite the pains and the pleasure of other minds: they never enquired what on any occasion they should have said or done, but wrote rather as beholders than partakers of human nature.[40]

The idea of the equality of the intellect, suggested by Bacon and substantiated by the Royal Society, had become, by the middle of the eighteenth century, the equality and generality of the emotions themselves. They were known, fixed and inevitable, the personal equivalents of the great moral and social truths to which everyone adhered.

The second statement concerns those truths themselves:

> Those writers who lay on the watch for novelty could have little hope of greatness; for great things cannot have escaped former observation. Their attempts were always analytick.

The great things, in fact, are self-evident: they are matters of observation—though I imagine Johnson means they are

[40] *Idem*, I, p. 20.

observed less by experimental devices than by common sense and humanity. Analysis, on the other hand, has nothing to do with either Truth (with a capital 'T') or with the true workings of the mind.

Perhaps this is what Eliot meant by the dissociation of sensibility. It is primarily a change in the way of thinking: no longer dialectics and verbal analysis, but factual observation and common sense. I suggested that behind this there was, because of the Civil War, a fear of argument as such. But there was, too, a fear of words, or rather of the potentiality of language. The motto of the Royal Society was *'Nullius in Verba'*. It comes, I am told, from Horace and is a refusal to accept prior authority: *'Nullius addictus jurare in verba magistri'* (Not bound to the words of any master). By it the Fellows of the Royal Society meant to show their clean break with mediaeval philosophy; the master, of course, was Aristotle. But as the tag appears abbreviated in the Society's coat-of-arms, the emphasis is on the verbal element of the old authorities. The implication is that the Society would not deal in words at all when it was possible to keep to things. It seems to me that the whole attitude of the Restoration to language was, in a way, an attempt to treat words *as* things: circumscribed by definitions, factual in their reference, simple in form, and meaning one thing only. That is why they wanted to set up a commission for reforming and regulating the language. This meant that, in philosophy, there was to be no more scholastic equivocation and logic-chopping and, in poetry, no more of the puns and polysyllabics of Cleveland and his strongliners. And this kind of distrustful circumscription of language went with another sign of the dissociation of sensibility I have already mentioned: the massive simplicity of the critical theory, which resolved poetic imagination into a mechanics of opposing forces, such as fancy and judgment.

But all these are merely signs of a deeper change; a change of the direction in which the imagination moved. It is implicit in Johnson's contrast between observation and analysis, or in the passage from Sprat I quoted earlier:

> The contemplation of (nature) draws our minds off from past, or present misfortunes,—makes them conquerors over things, in the greatest publick unhappiness: while the consideration of *Man,* and *humane affairs,* may affect us with a thousand disquiets.

The insistence on things and clarity, on ordered and prescribed observation, on great truths generally agreed upon, and on the equalization of the intellect and feelings, all this is part of a deliberate turning outwards of poetry, away from the mind and towards impersonal nature. What Eliot called the dissociation of sensibility, I would call the extroversion of the imagination. The other way was that of analysis. It meant, particularly in its degenerate forms, that words were turned in on themselves in endless equivocations, and arguments in endless dialectical sophistry. I do not think that the Restoration writers were ever willing to see it in anything but its degenerate shape. That is why, following Bacon and Hobbes, they all described Metaphysicians in the image of a spider spinning his web out of his own guts: the philosopher spinning abstractions out of his intellect.

But in doing so, they lost not merely Cleveland and the game of wit, but Donne and Herbert, writers who used logic to analyse vividly dramatized personal situations with complete fidelity to psychological realism, and who linked their analysis to the kind of intellectual themes which preoccupied their particular brand of tough intelligence. In place of all this the Restoration favoured a standardized pattern both for the feelings and for the occasion. That is why Dryden accused Donne of "perplexing the minds of the fair sex with nice speculations of philosophy, when he should engage their hearts, and entertain them with the softnesses of love".

Moreover, this determination to view language as though it were composed of a series of fixed and discreet units automatically did away with a whole area of imaginative potentiality: that tentative moulding of new metaphors and words to fit exactly the intricacies of the poet's emotion. This is what Middleton Murry meant by 'style', Leavis by his use of the word 'exploratory' and Eliot by the idea of 'dislocating words into meaning'. It is a quality associated most with Shakespeare and the Jacobean dramatists, but it is just as keenly present in King's 'Exequy', in the beginning of Lovelace's 'La Bella Bona-Roba', in the stanza I quoted from Herbert's 'The Flower' and in Donne at his most typical and best:

> wee understood
> Her by her sight; her pure, and eloquent blood
> Spoke in her cheekes, and so distinctly wrought,
> That one might almost say, her body thought.

This tentative realization of the potentialities of a feeling through the potentialities of language was done for directly the Royal Society set about treating words like the clear, distinct and circumscribed facts of natural experiment.

The School of Donne was dismissed, then, because the old dialectical ways of thinking on which it relied were abandoned. And this went with the rejection of the intellect, and of everything that Carew implied when he called Donne

> a King, that rul'd as hee thought fit
> The universall Monarchy of wit.

For the Restoration, intellectual brillance led in one direction to deliberate obscurity, over-subtlety and dispute; in the other, to mental pride, which meant fanaticism. The way between, safe and open to all, was that of impersonal experimental knowledge:

> Transgression of the *Law* is *Idolatry:* The *reason* of mens contemning all *Jurisdiction* and *Power,* proceeds from their Idolizing of their own *Wit:* They make their own Prudence omnipotent; they suppose themselves *infallible;* they set up their own *Opinions,* and worship them. But this vain *Idolatry* will inevitably fall before *Experimental Knowledge;* which as it is an *enemy* to all manner of fals *superstititions,* so especially to that of mens *adoring themselves* and *their own Fancies.*[41]

Sprat is talking, as it happens, of the cult of the Puritan conscience, and its disrupting spiritual arrogance. But his criticisms are substantially the same as those made of the Schoolmen and of the Metaphysical poets: when the individual took too much upon his own unaided powers he ended, sooner or later, in disaster. Bacon had shown the dangers that beset theory when it bowed before wit, and had suggested a remedy; Hobbs had seen the problem as a threat to society; Sprat, with the Royal Society behind him, had confidently and with relief celebrated the triumph of Nature over Wit. There could be no compromise. Hence the apotheosis of 'things', the rejection of analysis, the equalization of the intellect and the freezing of language. They all led, inevitably, to the rejection of the style of the School of Donne.

[41] *History of the Royal Society,* III, xxxix, p. 430.

APPENDIXES

Appendix I

DONNE'S CIRCLE

THE foundation of Donne's circle was laid at Oxford, where Donne went when he was about twelve; he matriculated on October 23rd, 1584, and went down two years later. There he formed lasting friendships with Sir Henry Wotton, John Hoskyns and Sir Richard Baker. Wotton and Hoskyns were at Winchester and New College together; Wotton matriculated on June 5th, 1584, Hoskyns on March 5th, 1585.[1] Wotton moved on to Donne's college, Hart Hall, where he shared rooms with Baker, who later wrote:

> The Trojan horse was not fuller of heroic Grecians than King James his reign was full of men excellent in all kinds of learning. And here I desire the reader's leave to remember two of my acquaintance, the one was Mr John Donne, who leaving Oxford, lived at the Inns of Court, not dissolute, but very neat; a great visitor of ladies. . . . The other was Henry Wotton (mine old acquaintance also, as having been fellow-pupils and chamber-fellows in Oxford divers years together). This gentleman was employed by King James in embassage to Venice; and indeed the kingdom afforded no fitter man for matching the capriciousness of Italian wits; a man of so able dexterity with his pen, that he hath done himself much wrong, and the Kingdom more, in leaving no more of his writings behind him.[2]

Wotton has several good minor poems to his credit, which survive in *Reliquiae Wottonianae*, 1651. He admired the 'Dorique delicacy' of the songs in *Comus* and was to have

---

[1] See Louise Brown Osborn, *The Life, Letters, and Writings of John Hoskyns*, 1937, p. 5.

[2] Sir Richard Baker, *Chronicles of the Kings of England*, 1643; 1674 edition, pp. 446-7. Quoted by Logan Pearsall Smith, *The Life and Letters of Sir Henry Wotton*, 2 vols., Oxford, 1907, II, p. 461.

143

written a life of Donne as a preface to the collected sermons, but died before doing so.[3]

John Hoskyns, according to Aubrey, "had a booke of
Poemes, neatly written by one of his Clerkes, bigger than
Dr Donne's Poemes, which his sonn Benet lent to he knowes
not who, about 1653, and could never heare of it since".[4]
One of them, 'Absense, hear thou my protestation', survived
in a manuscript belonging to Donne and was ascribed to
him in the eighteenth century.[5] Another was written *alternis
vicibus* with Wotton 'riding on the way'.[6] Ben Jonson, says
Aubrey,

> called him *father*. Sir Benet told me that one time desir-
> ing Mr Johnson to adopt him for his sonne, No, said
> he, I dare not; 'tis honour enough for me to be your
> Brother: I was your Father's sonne, and 'twas he that
> polished me.[7]

His right to polish even Jonson is proved by his *Directions
for Speech and Style,* one of the most intelligent writing
manuals of the time. It is based on the ideas of Lipsius,
one of the 'Attic' writers, and is almost the only place where
the Metaphysical conceit is taken account of:

> It is true we study according to the predominancy of
> courtly inclinations: whilst mathematics were in re-
> quests, all our similitudes came from lines, circles and
> angles; while moral philosophy is now a while spoken
> of, it is rudeness not to be sententious.[8]

Jonson, incidentally, thought the *Directions* intelligent
enough to be worth transcribing: sections of it were found

---

[3] Izaak Walton wrote the life of Donne in Wotton's place and also
wrote a life of Wotton. Apart from Logan Pearsall Smith's definitive
work on Wotton, there is also an excellent brief biography in Helen
Gardner's *The Metaphysical Poets,* 1957, p. 320. See also the valuable
cultural analysis of Wotton's circle: L. C. Knights, 'On the Social
Background of Metaphysical Poetry', *Scrutiny,* XIII, 1945, pp. 37-52.

[4] John Aubrey, *Brief Lives,* ed. Oliver Lawson Dick, 1950, p. 170.

[5] See H. J. C. Grierson, *The Poems of John Donne,* 2 vols., Oxford,
1912, II, p. cli.

[6] *Reliquiae Wottonianae,* 1651, p. 517, and Osborn, *loc. cit.,*
pp. 211-12.

[7] *Loc. cit.* p. 169.

[8] John Hoskyns, *Directions for Speech and Style,* c. 1599-1600,
ed. Hoyt H. Hudson, Princeton, 1935, p. 39.

among his manuscripts and even printed as his own in *Timber*.[9]

Sir Richard Baker's writings all came after Donne's death and at the end of his own mildly distinguished political career, when he became entangled in the debts of his wife's family and was imprisoned in the Fleet in 1635. When they did come, they were intelligent and substantial. He even tried his hand at a verse translation of Cato.[10]

All three friends went on to the Inns of Court. Wotton was with Donne on Essex's expeditions to Cadiz and the Azores in 1596 and 1597. Donne was Member of Parliament for Brackley in 1601; Baker was M.P. for Arundel in 1593 and for East Grinstead in 1597; Hoskyns was M.P. for Hereford in 1604.

Other writers at Oxford may have been attracted to this nucleus of wits. The epigrammatists, Thomas Bastard and John Owen were there at the same time. Both, like Wotton and Hoskyns, were Winchester-New College men. Donne gives no sign of having known either, but then they did not go on to the Inns of Court. Yet Bastard contributed to a poetical *débat* between Bacon, Wotton and Donne,[11] and his book of epigrams, *Chrestoleros*, entered in the Stationers' Register in 1598, contains poems to Essex, Egerton and Wotton, the circle Donne was moving in at that time.[12] As for Owen: Hoskyns apparently kept up with him. He wrote him two epigrams which were printed in the third edition of Owen's *Epigrammes* in 1607.[13] Owen also knew Donne's friend Sir John Roe.[14] And both were friendly with Sir Benjamin Rudyerd. Rudyerd himself did not arrive from Winchester to St John's, Oxford, until Donne had gone down; he matriculated on January 15th, 1587-8. But he was

---

[9] See *Ben Jonson*, ed. C. H. Herford and Percy Simpson, 11 vols., Oxford, 1925-52, VIII, pp. 628-33, XI, pp. 274-8.

[10] For full details of his career and writings, see the *Dictionary of National Biography*.

[11] See H. J. C. Grierson, 'Bacon's Poem, "The World": Its date and Relation to Certain Other Poems', *Modern Language Review*, VI, 1911, pp. 145-56. It took place probably between October 1597 and April 1598.

[12] Thomas Bastard, *Poems English and Latin*, ed. Alexander B. Grosart, 1880.

[13] Reprinted by Osborn, *loc. cit.* pp. 209-10.

[14] Roe and Hoskyns wrote Latin epitaphs on Owen; they are printed by Osborn, *loc. cit.*, p. 294, from MS. Harley 3910.

at the Middle Temple with Hoskyns,[15] where he was busy, like the others, in building himself a reputation as a wit. He seems to have succeeded: Ben Jonson wrote him three epigrams, numbers cxxi-cxxiii, all very laudatory. He was prominent in the Temple festivities. His poems were printed in 1660 together with the Earl of Pembroke's, his intimate friend and relation by marriage.[16] Later in life he became a prominent politician. But it is no more than probable that Donne knew these men; he mentions none of them by name.

The next extension of his circle of acquaintance came when he entered Lincoln's Inn on May 6th, 1592.[17] This was the beginning of the poems, the period when Donne was perfecting his style and wit.[18] His closest friend, with whom he shared chambers, was Christopher Brook, who, like Donne, later became a Bencher and Reader at Lincoln's Inn. Brook, whose works were substantial enough to have been edited by Grosart,[19] had Selden, Jonson, Drayton, Wither, Davies of Hereford and William Browne among the admirers of his poetry.[20] His brother Samuel Brook performed Donne's secret marriage ceremony while Christopher gave the bride away.[21] Samuel later became Chaplain to Prince Henry, to James I and Charles I, was Professor of

[15] Admitted April 18th, 1590, three years before Hoskyns, who stayed on at Oxford. Called to the Bar, October 24th, 1600. See *A Catalogue of Notable Middle Templars* by John Hutchinson, 1902, pp. 210-11. The *D.N.B.* makes a number of mistakes about his early career.

[16] A song of Pembroke's, 'Soules joy, now I am gone', and a poetical exchange between him and Rudyerd were printed as Donne's work from 1633 to 1669; see Grierson, I, pp. 429-32, and II, pp. cxxxv-vi.

[17] Sir Edmund Gosse believes that between leaving Oxford and entering Lincoln's Inn, Donne transferred to Cambridge; see *The Life and Letters of John Donne*, 2 vols., 1899, I, p. 19. Had he done so he might have met Christopher and Samuel Brook before going to Lincoln's Inn.

[18] R. C. Bald dates the verse letters to B.B., S.B., T.W. ('Haste thee, harsh verse . . .'), E.G. and I.L. from the end of 1592 until August 1594. See 'Donne's Early Verse Letters', *Huntington Library Quarterly*, XV, 1952, pp. 283-9.

[19] Christopher Brook, *Complete Poems*, ed. Alexander B. Grosart, *Miscellanies of the Fuller Worthies Library*, vol. IV, 1872.

[20] See Anthony à Wood, *Fasti Oxonienses*, ed. Philip Bliss, 1815, Pt. I, p. 403. William Browne dedicated Eclogue V of *The Shepherd's Pipe*, 1614, to him, and praised him in *Brittania's Pastorals*, 1625. See his *Poems*, ed. Gordon Goodwin, 2 vols., 1894, II, pp. 143 ff., and I, p. 240.

[21] See Gosse; *loc. cit.*, I, p. 98.

Divinity at Gresham College, 1612-19, and Master of Trinity College, Cambridge, in 1629.[22]

Then there was Rowland Woodward. Donne wrote him verse letters and presented him with a copy of *Pseudo-Martyr* in 1610; he was in Wotton's embassy in Venice in 1605 and ended his life in a minor position at Court.[23] Other of Donne's verse letters went to Rowland's kinsman, Thomas Woodward, who is probably the person of that name who matriculated at Clare College, Cambridge, in 1593,[24] entered Lincoln's Inn in October 1597,[25] was called to the bar in 1605 and later became a Bencher and Reader.[26] If B. B. is, as Mr. R. C. Bald argues, Beaupré Bell, then he was the son of the Chief Baron of the Exchequer and left Cambridge to join Donne at Lincoln's Inn in 1595.[27] There was also Everard Gilpin, the satirist, of Emanuel College, Cambridge, and Gray's Inn.[28] Unlike the others, Gilpin published. His *Skialetheia* appeared in 1598. The beginning of his '5th Satyre' is an elaboration of the first twelve lines of Donne's 'Satyre I'. The imitation, in fact, is so close that it is hard to decide whether it is intended as an act of homage to the leader of a group of writers, or he presumed that Donne's work was so little known that his plagiarism would pass unnoticed. It remains the earliest surviving evidence of Donne's influence.[29]

Sir John Roe and Sir William Cornwallis joined Donne after the Cadiz and Azores Expeditions, when he was Egerton's secretary at York House. Both were at Queen's College, Oxford; both served with Essex in Ireland in 1599,

[22] Grierson, II, p. 170. His poem, 'On Tears', is printed in Hannah's *Courtly Poets* and in *Reliquial Wottonianae*.

[23] He was Deputy Master of Ceremonies from 1630 until his death some time before April 1636. See M. C. Deas, 'A Note on Rowland Woodward, the friend of Donne', *Review of English Studies*, VII, 1931, pp. 454-7.

[24] J. and J. A. Venn, *Alumni Cantabrigienses*, Cambridge, 1922, I, p. 461.

[25] The *Records of the Honourable Society of Lincoln's Inn, Admissions*, 1896, I, p. 125.

[26] *Idem, Black Books*, I, pp. 96, 217, 237. An entry on p. 450 shows that he was still alive in 1624.

[27] R. C. Bald, *loc. cit.*, p. 284.

[28] R. E. Bennett, 'John Donne and Everard Gilpin', *Review of English Studies*, XV, 1939, pp. 66-72.

[29] See Grierson, II, p. 105; Bennett, *loc. cit.*, p. 72; W. Milgate, 'The Early References to John Donne', *Notes and Queries*, CXCV, 1950, p. 229.

where, like Sir Henry Goodyer, Cornwallis was knighted; both imitated Donne. Roe's poems—he was a friend of Jonson—were sometimes ascribed to Donne; they are good copies of his rougher, cynical style.[30] Cornwallis, who was also the first English imitator of Montaigne, dedicated his encomium of Richard III to Donne, whilst his 'Various facetious pieces written . . . in the yeere of our Lord Christ 1600 beinge the 22th yeere of his age'[31] are, like much of Donne's younger writing, paradoxical and full of obscure, knowing references to the Greek philosophers. Both were literary amateurs: Roe was a soldier, Cornwallis a politician.[32]

Sir Francis Wooley seems first to have met Donne on the expedition to the Azores. But the friendship ripened since Wooley was Egerton's step-son and was at York House when Donne was the Lord Chancellor's secretary. After Donne's marriage and disgrace, it was Wooley who rallied round and, as Walton says, "intreated them to a cohabitation with him" at "Pirford in Surry".[33] Sir Tobie Mathew, the friend of Bacon, was at Gray's Inn at the turn of the century and became an M.P. the same year as Donne. He was also a lifelong friend of Wotton and Goodyer.[34]

Sir Henry Goodyer, Middle Templar, was perhaps Donne's most intimate friend. Donne wrote him a weekly letter during the lean years in Pyrford, Mitcham and London, and during Goodyer's own difficulties, Donne may have lent him money and even wrote his letters for him.[35] He showed Donne hospitality at his country house, Polesworth, where he also entertained Jonson and Drayton, and probably introduced Donne to the Countess of Bedford.[36]

---

[30] See Grierson, II, pp. cxxix-xxxv, where there is also a short biography of Roe.

[31] MS. Tanner 169, fol. 132-7. They have been printed by R. E. Bennett, *Harvard Studies and Notes in Philology and Literature*, XIII, 1931.

[32] For the evidence on Cornwallis, see P. B. Whitt, 'New Light on Sir William Cornwallis', *Review of English Studies*, 1932, pp. 155-69; also letters by Whitt, C. E. Avery and R. E. Bennett in *The Times Literary Supplement*, 1930, Oct. 23, Nov. 6, Nov. 20, Dec. 4.

[33] Walton's *Lives*, with an Introduction and Notes by S. B. Carter, 1951, p. 14. Also Gosse, *loc. cit.*, I, p. 120.

[34] David Mathew, *Sir Tobie Mathew*, 1950, pp. 29-30, 56; also *A Collection of Letters, made by Sir Tobie Mathew Kt.* 1660.

[35] R. E. Bennett, 'Sir Henry Goodyere and Donne's Letters' *Modern Language Notes*, LXIII, 1948, pp. 38-43.

[36] See B. H. Newdigate, *Michael Drayton and His Circle*, Oxford, 1941, pp. 81-3. Also Grierson, II, pp. 144-5.

(i) ATTACKS ON DONNE

ALTHOUGH writing *Satyres,* Donne had nothing to do with
the contemporary satiric wars. His friend Gilpin, however,
plagiarized from Donne in order to join battle with Marston
and Hall (see Appendix I).

Christopher Brook's friend, William Browne of Tavistock,
wrote quite a good poem which begins:

> Poore silly soule, thou striv'st in vayne to know
> Whither I know, or love, who thou lov'st soe.
> Since my affecōn ever secrett tryed
> Blossoms like ferne, and seeds still unespied.

In a late Bodley manuscript, from which I am quoting, this
poem is entitled: 'An Answere to Dr Donnes curse Who
ever guesses etc—'.[1] There is no indication of any reply by
Donne.

Michael Drayton, who was a very professional poet indeed and may have had Donne to thank for losing the favour of the Countess of Bedford, has three bursts of in-
vective—in *The Owle,* 1604, Song XXI of *Polyolbion,* 1612,
and the *Epistle to Reynolds,* 1627—whose object may be
Donne. But the evidence is indecisive.[2]

---

[1] MS. Rawlinson, Poet. 147, fol. 83. The MS. is dated 1647 and
ascribed to 'H. S.', whom I cannot identify. The poem is printed from
well-authenticated sources in *The Poems of William Brown of Tavistock,* ed. Gordon Goodwin, 1894, 2 vols., II, p. 197.

[2] See Raymond Jenkins, 'Drayton's Relation to the School of
Donne', *Publications of the Modern Language Association of America,*
XXXVIII, 1923, pp. 557-87; R. W. Short, 'Ben Jonson in Drayton's
Poems', *Review of English Studies,* XVI, 1940, pp. 149-58; answered
by Percy Simpson and Kathleen Tillotson, *Review of English Studies,*
XVI, 1940, pp. 303-6; summed up by B. H. Newdigate, *Michael
Drayton and His Circle,* Oxford, 1941, pp. 63-9.

(ii)   DONNE AND THE MISCELLANIES

Donne contributed only to *Coryat's Crudities,* 1611, and to Joshua Sylvester's *Lachrymae Lachrymarum,* 1613. In the former his contribution follows immediately those of the titled writers. Coryat was associated with the dinners at the Mitre and Mermaid, which Donne also attended.[3] To the latter he contributed the 'Elegie upon . . . Prince Henry', about which Jonson told Drummond 'That Donne said to him he wrott that Epitaph on Prince Henry, Look to me, Faith, to match Sir Ed: Herbert in obscurenesse'.[4]

Grierson points out that Francis Davison, sometime after 1608, tried to get some of Donne's poems for his *Poetical Rhapsody,* 1602, 1608, 1611, 1621.[5] There is no indication that he succeeded. All that survives is a note in his hand where, under the heading 'Manuscripts to get' he lists 'Satyres, Elegies, Epigrams, etc., by John Don. Q$^{re.}$ same from Eleaz. Hodgson, and Ben Jonson'.[6] Hodgson was much like Donne's other associates: he was an M.A. of Oxford and Cambridge, became an M.D. of Padua, an F.R.C.P. and one of the most eminent physicians in London.[7]

[3] See I. A. Shapiro, 'The "Mermaid Club" ', *Modern Language Review,* XLV, 1950, pp. 6-17. This article is essential for understanding Donne's later audience.

[4] *The Conversations of Ben Jonson and William Drummond of Hawthornden,* 1619; *Ben Jonson,* ed. C. H. Herford and Percy Simpson, Oxford, 1925-1952, 11 vols., I, p. 136.

[5] Grierson, II, pp. lvi-lvii.

[6] See Francis Davison, *Poetical Rhapsody,* ed. A. H. Bullen, 2 vols., 1890, I, p. liii.

[7] J. and J. A. Venn, *Alumni Cantabrigienses,* Cambridge, 1922, I, p. 384.

INDEX

153

The SIGNET CLASSIC SHAKESPEARE

Superlatively edited paperbound volumes of the complete works of Shakespeare are now being added to the Signet Classic list. Under the general editorship of Sylvan Barnet, Chairman of the English Department of Tufts University, each volume features a general introduction by Dr. Barnet; special Introduction and Notes by an eminent Shakespearean scholar; critical commentary from past and contemporary authorities, and when possible, the original source material, in its entirety or in excerpt, on which Shakespeare based his work. Among the volumes already available, at 50¢ each, are: